More Birds
Than Bullets

My Life with Birds

Geoffrey McMullan

Cover Illustration by Cliff Wright
All illustrations by Geoffrey McMullan
Chapter 9 Illustration by unknown artists

Printed in the United Kingdom

First Printing, 2020

ISBN: 978-0-9576181-4-5 (Paperback)
ISBN: 978-0-9576181-3-8 (eBook)

Pathfinder UK
6 Tray Lane
Atherington, Umberleigh
Devon, EX37 9HY

www.pathfinder-uk.com

I dedicate this book to the birds, places, and people who were an important part of my experiences, and to the amazing people I served with; especially to those who are no longer with us.

It was an honour.

Service Record

UNITS SERVED

Woolwich Training Depot		1975 — 1975
40th	Field Regiment R. A.	1975 — 1981
27th	Field Regiment R. A.	1981 — 1986
49th	Field Regiment R. A.	1986 — 1990
2nd	Field Regiment R. A.	1990 — 1991
49th	Field Regiment R. A.	1991 — 1992
26th	Field Regiment R. A.	1992 — 1996
Woolwich Training Depot		1996 — 1997

TOURS

Northern Ireland	1977 — 1978
Cyprus	1982 — 1982
Canada	1989 — 1989
	1990 — 1990
	1992 — 1992
Saudi Arabia, Iraq & Kuwait	1990 — 1991
Kuwait	1991 — 1991
Falklands Islands	1993 — 1994
	1995 — 1995
Former Yugoslavia	1996 — 1996

DECORATIONS, MEDALS & AWARDS

British Empire Medal (Conservation & Anglo-German Relations)
General Service Medal (Northern Ireland & Kuwait)
Gulf War Medal (Saudi Arabia, Iraq & Kuwait)
NATO Medal (Former Yugoslavia)
Commendation (Commander Royal Artillery – Gulf War)

OTHER MEDALS

Saudi Medal (Issued by the Kingdom of Saudi Arabia)
Kuwait Medal (Issued by the Kingdom of Kuwait)

Contents

Preface

For year's friends have encouraged me to write about my birding experiences. Until recently I have resisted it for various reasons, then I thought it might be fun to put pen to paper. 'More Birds Than Bullets' is not just as the title suggests, there is more to it than that, it can be seen as a metaphor for life's experiences. I struggled with how I should go about writing it, should it be factual, or should it be like a novel? In the end I decided to write about my experiences from my time in the army through to civilian life, I have included some facts about birds, and rather than write out a long list of the birds I have seen, I concentrate instead on a small number of birds in slightly more detail. As you come across the birds and the places mentioned in this book it is worth looking them up on the internet to hear and to see them in their full glory and I have limited the military jargon for those of you who may have no experience of the way military personnel speak.

The stories are not in chronological order and I have avoided dates, unit names, and other details unless it is necessary as part of the story. My aim is to give you an insight into my world as a birder, the stories are true and based on my experiences. I have changed names to protect people, unless it shows them in a good light as it's not my intention to cause harm to anyone. I will share with you some of my background and my relationship with birds, people, and the countries I have visited, and how they formed my understanding of my world by concluding with my transition from civilian, to military and back to civilian life. I hope you find it amusing, informative, unbelievable and maybe even shocking.

After leaving boarding school in Cheltenham, which is where I discovered birds for the first time, I attended college in Ware, Hertfordshire where I studied Commercial Art. I left college having decided not to take my exams, against the tutors and my dad's best efforts to keep me in. I actually got into college based solely on my artwork; some of which is in this book normally you were required to have several A and O-Levels, of which I had none.

After leaving college, I focused on getting work and during this time birds had taken a back seat. I moved around from job to job not settling on any of them, in those days you could leave one job, cross the road and get another job the same day. A CV was not needed, in fact they had not even been thought of back then. I worked as a salesman for several menswear companies, and a machinist making women's coats, this is where I learnt sign language. I went onto silk screen printing, then tool-setting. One day while bending bits of metal, I decided I had had enough and on a whim, I joined the British Army aged eighteen. I caught the bus from work, went to the recruitment office in Old Harlow, Essex, and signed on; I was given a small bible, the Queen's Shilling (both of which I still have), and a day's wages. I then went on to serve for twenty-two years and four days in the Royal Regiment of Artillery.

It was not until I was posted to Germany from training in Woolwich, London that I once again came into contact with birds, it's from this period that my birding flourished. After leaving the army I had several jobs before heading to Belize with Raleigh International as their logistics manager. Returning from there and several jobs later, I found my ideal job; it was in a rehab where my boss put me through University at London Southbank.

Aged fifty, I qualified in Addiction Psychology and Counselling and I went on to focus my work in Nature-based Counselling which involved aspects of bushcraft, tracking and bird language as part of the therapeutic process. If you take away all the trades I learnt in the army, the only civilian qualification I have is a Masters in Addiction Psychology and Counselling. I learnt a lot in the army; and on so many different levels as well.

An important aspect of this book is the people I had the privilege to meet; I thank them all for their help, support and guidance while travelling in their country, without which I could have ended up in real trouble. I would also like to thank the following people for their input: Cliff Wright my good friend who painted the original cover designs of Harry Potter and the Chamber of Secrets and Harry Potter and the Prisoner of Azkaban. I had to drop that one in; and for the excellent drawing on the cover to this book.

To Lt Col Roger Dickey R. A. for allowing me to use 'More Birds Than Bullets' as the title of this book; and to those closest and dearest to me for their help and support during the creating of this book, to Badger for casting a non-military eye over the text and giving me honest and sincere feedback. Richard for the fun times birding together and to the folks from CAOS, sorry I mean the AOS.

To the men and women, I have served with (particularly 127 Dragon Battery; especially to my men who were not only my backbone, but are my friends and each and everyone holds a special place in my heart), it was a real honour. I indicate within the text the brothers in arms who are no longer with us, with the letters RIP (Rest in Peace); when it is my time to crossover, I will see you at the bar and mine is a Guinness. Cheers. Thanks to my friends who allowed me to take part in their projects, in no particular order Karl Loske, Wolf Leader, Andreas Kämpfer, Mark Michaels, Martjan Lammertink. To, Peter Hoffmann, for his friendship and his support while we took on the task of building the Zachariassee Nature Reserve. I am grateful for Zachariassee being in my life, it helped me in so many ways and without doubt it is one of the jewels in my crown. I especially would like to thank Martjan Lammertink, Tulio Dornas. Tim Cowley and Brian Stech for the use of their photographs in this book.

To my friends for posing questions, while challenging, they helped me to explore my personal feelings, which in turn has helped me to understand the importance of birds in my life; in particular woodpeckers. Thanks to Mark Cocker for agreeing to write the foreword, Jon Young for bringing Bird Language into my field of view and Sam Pearce (SWATT Books) for taking on the task of setting this book up for publishing.

Not forgetting my lovely daughters Janine and Nickie Sara for putting up with their Dad's birding throughout the years and to my beautiful granddaughter Josefine, who has got it all to come; and finally, I am grateful for the wonderful, powerful, and amazing

Close Encounters of the Bird Kind

Foreword

Mark Cocker – Author of Birds and People

Brought up in a land of sectarian conflict and for the first half of his working life a soldier in the British Army, Geoffrey McMullan is, I suppose, your average warrior. As he himself loves to tell us, he is six foot four and built like the proverbial shithouse door. But Geoffrey has a softer side as well as a secret inner life that he exposes among all the rambunctious, globe-trotting adventure of this humour-filled memoir. He is one for the birds. Give him a Heart-spotted Woodpecker, it seems, and this great big bear of a man is moved to his soul. Birds? I hear one or two readers ask. Isn't that a bit, well, cissy? What can be so moving or special about birds?

The truth is that Geoffrey's passion is both ancient and universal. To the Sufi mystics of central Asia, God was sometimes known as 'the unnamed bird'. For Native Americans – the Cheyenne and Lakota peoples of the American plains – the mythic 'thunderbird' was central to their spiritual lives. In the Andes the Quechua held the condor sacred for thousands of years. Zeus the preeminent deity of the ancient Greeks was represented as an eagle. So too was Jupiter for the Romans and their priests, at the death of an emperor, would release one of these great birds of prey at the funeral pyre itself.

Far stranger was the significance that the Romans accorded to their sacred chickens. It involved a form of augury – a word that meant literally 'watching birds' – and required a state official known as a *pullarius* to note the manner in which the fowls foraged, but also the sound and force of the grain as it spilt it on the ground. No political or military decision could be taken unless the auspices had been consulted.

Assemblies of the people, war levies, great affairs of state – all could be put off if the birds withheld their approval. Aah, I hear you say, but that is all in the past, we are through with all that superstitious bird stuff. Not quite. When you next send one, look closely at your Valentine's cards (doves) or Christmas cards (doves and now robins) and chances are they will feature birds. The truth is that these creatures are central images for our most cherished ideals – love beauty, inner peace.

Geoffrey McMullan knew this instinctively. In his book he describes a moving moment when, as a small boy, to fend off the casual violence of his boarding school, he alighted on a woodpecker on the lawn outside the dining room window. To that troubled child the bird was a source of peace and comfort.

He goes on in *More Birds than Bullets* to show how this understanding has blossomed into a lifelong form of personal therapy. In the second half of his working life, as a teacher on the healing power of the natural world, Geoffrey is again summoning the birds but to demonstrate to others their uplifting potential.

Encounters of the feathered kind are written into the DNA of Geoffrey's autobiography. And he tells us of adventures everywhere – Thailand, Yemen, Namibia, Mexico, you name it – in pursuit of nature, especially after his beloved owls and woodpeckers. You'll even find a story about an unlikely-sounding species called a Heart-spotted Woodpecker, which he claims to have seen. And who am I to doubt him. He is, after all, a great bear of a man, six-foot-four and, as he has told us before, built like a ....

My Travel Tips

I have had countless experiences when travelling, from the UK to Germany, the Middle East to Bosnia and many lands in between covering around 73 countries to date. In fact, I did so much travelling in the latter part of my military career, people use to say that, I put in a leave application to come back to work. I travelled so much, that on one occasion I returned from South America, just in time for my dine out (leaving party), arriving, after the meal and just as the Battery Commander stood up to give his speech to those that were leaving the army; I believe this to be a rare event. To aid my traveling experience; I have a few things that I like to do, they are as follows:

1. I have my get out of jail cards, namely my passport and credit card.
2. I never look at a map in public, especially in Cities.
3. I always maintain an air of confidence, even if I don't feel confident.
4. If I like a place, I stay. If I don't like it, I move onto the next place, which I have pre-planned.
5. I **ALWAYS** heed local advice, even if it means dipping out on lots of cracking birds.
6. I carry a dummy wallet which contains the following:
   a. Monopoly money
   b. False dollars bought through the internet
   c. Low value legal tender that cannot be exchanged
   d. Cardboard credit cards; from junk mail. To the would-be thief, at first glance the cards and notes look like the real thing.

7. I print on a large card all my details. I place one in each of my bags, in case I get separated from my luggage.

8. If my train, bus or plane breaks down or is delayed, I get my field guide out, order a beer and relax. There is nothing I can do about it. So, I let others fix the problem while I enjoy my beer and the birds in my field guide.

***

5a While I feel all these tips are important, I would suggest that this is the most important one. Always listen to local advice, it is better to be safe than sorry.

6a I have never had to use my dummy wallet; it might be because I am 6' 4" and built like a brick outhouse. Although joking aside, I suspect it is more to do with appearing relaxed and confident. However, if I do get held up, they get my dummy wallet and while they are running away, I am having it away on my toes in the opposite direction before they rumble me.

7a Anyone who finds my bags now have my address, phone number, e-mail address and other relevant information to return my bags. I do not rely on the tag around the baggage handle as it may become dislodged in transit.

CHAPTER 1

Woodpeckers

I can still see it now, just as if it was yesterday. Aged eleven, I was sitting at the breakfast table looking out of the window in an all boy's boarding school. It was a summer morning, the rain had stopped, and I was not anticipating a good day, or even a different day. Boarding school was not a happy place.

Then something caught my eye, as I watched it driving its beak deep into the lawn; I could see a bright yellow rump on a green body with black, white and red head markings. It was my first ever woodpecker, actually it was the first time that I had even noticed birds. It took me to another world, a world that was safer than the one I was living in.

There were no unreasonable rules, no labels like 'maladjusted', no bloodied nose delivered by a teacher, no food being forced into my mouth because I did not like it and no cat o' nine tails at the hands of the Principle. When you receive the cat o' nine tails you hardly feel it, but it was very painful when you tried sitting down afterwards. I guess that is where the expression comes from; you will not be able to sit down for a week afterwards. I am not sure that it lasted for a week, but certainly it did for a few days. This nine-tailed whip originated as an implement for severe physical punishment, notably in the Royal Navy and the British Army.

It was not until many years later that I realised the comfort I derived from seeing the Green Woodpecker on the lawn that day. I felt safe in what was an <u>extremely</u> abusive environment. The amazing colours, the shape and the movement of its body, were pure magic to me.

I believe this was the beginning of my love affair with birds, particularly with Woodpeckers. Oddly enough it was a teacher who was German, that got me interested in birds. He encouraged me to join the Young Ornithologists Club (YOC), which was the junior wing of the Royal Society for the Protection of Birds (RSBP). This was the very same man who had grabbed me around my neck from behind, dragged me from my desk and strangled me until I was close to passing out. I think it was because I called him a fat German.

I would often head for the woods behind the large gardens of this stately home, to gain access to the hide, which we built out of an old chicken coop. I would sit watching the birds, having a fag (cigarette) that I had taken from a packet I had hidden behind a brick, in the longest garden wall I have ever seen.

Back then there were several ways to get cigarettes, one was I would play up in class, and as a punishment I got sent to work with the gardeners who would give me a packet of Woodbines. I have to say, working with them was not a punishment as I always found time to watch birds in the garden. The other way was to sneak out at night and make our way to the local woods, once there we changed out of our school uniform, into civilian clothes and hid our uniform in bags for when we returned.

Sometimes we would hear Tawny Owls calling as we changed. Three of us would head for Churchdown, a nearby small village and here we would raid the wooden cigarette machine. The trick we used in order to get the fags was, to pay for one packet, then having removed that packet we would hold a matchstick on top of the drawer and slowly close it. This allowed the next packet to drop down without the drawer locking. We would take a few packets, well okay a bit more than a few.

On one occasion, as we returned, we saw a car parked along an overgrown track that led up to the school. As we walked past it, we noticed that the windows were all steamed up, we knew the car belonged to a male teacher and with him was the female teacher who was on shift that night too. In the morning I got into a dispute with the teacher concerned, I let it out of the bag that I had seen him in his car up to no good. I was rewarded with a bloody nose, having been punched by the teacher. After, leaving boarding school, birding was to take a back seat for a few years while I attended art collage. I later joined the British Army and did my training at Woolwich.

It was not until my posting to Germany in 1975 that I reconnected with birds, and it was here I encountered my second woodpecker.

This bird made a lasting impression on me and became my number one bird. I was out walking in the woods close to my house in Ummeln, Bielefeld, when I heard an unusual and unique sound.

It came closer and closer, I looked up and there flying right above me was a magnificent bird. It was simple in colour but quite powerful in its presence, as big as a crow with a strong looking ivory coloured beak standing out from its all black plumage, on its head was a bright red cap. It was a Black Woodpecker and the unique sound I heard was its flight call. Having lain dormant, the phoenix within was once again reignited and my interest in birds has been burning ever since.

One of my favourite moments with this woodpecker was when I was in a beech forest. The large trees were well-spaced apart, this afforded excellent views to observe the Black Woodpecker in flight. As I walked, in the distance I heard its flight call reverberating as it travelled deep from within the forest on the early fresh crisp morning. As it made its way towards me, the other bird songs seemed to fade away in the presence of this stunning bird. There was something very special about being the only person to witness this woodpecker in that moment.

Recently, I was asked why it is that I get extremely excited about seeing woodpeckers and yet when I see a different new species of bird my excitement does not seem as strong. As we talked about this, I came to a realisation where I was able to connect my feelings of immense joy back to the time, I was sitting at the breakfast table in boarding school.

We were on exercise (manoeuvres) in the hinterland of the German countryside; our job was to coordinate the regiments fire missions; therefore, it was important to maintain communications. One morning at dawn, I left the Fire Direction Centre (FDC) to check on the 27ft Larkspur telescopic radio mast. It was a horrible thing to work with especially during the winter, there were no hydraulics on this baby, not like today. Often without warning, it would collapse in on itself; and if you were not quick enough it would take chunks out of your hands, a painful experience indeed.

With the mast sorted, I returned to the FDC. The sun had just come up, its rays penetrating between the trees warmed my body, taking the edge off the cold I was feeling. As I approached the FDC, I became aware of movement high up in a Beech Tree directly above our Command Post (CP). I looked up and saw a large woodpecker's nest hole. I could see a blue stain on the bark directly below the hole and I knew that it had been caused by the woodpecker's tail rubbing against the bark as it excavated its nest hole. It had to be a Black Woodpecker's nest, going by the size of the hole, and the distance the stain was from it. I was about to enter the CP when I looked up again and spotted an ivorybill, glistening in the sunlight as its beak protruded from the hole, it was indeed a Black Woodpecker. Judging by its short-repeated calls of 'kiyak', it was clear we were disturbing it with our vehicle parked directly under its nest and a 500-Watt generator making a lot of noise.

Even though we had dug it into the ground to dampen the sound and reduce the distance it would travel from our location. At that time, I was a gunner (private), and even though I thought he might rip my head off for having the audacity to speak to him, I approached the Adjutant (a captain), the officer in charge of the FDC. I asked him if we could move the FDC. Startled, he looked at me and asked why.

I showed him the agitated bird with half of its body now hanging out of the nest while still calling frantically. I said that the male (males sit throughout the night) could abandon the eggs or young if we stay here. He looked back at me, he paused and then said, "We will move after this fire mission". Thank God for that I thought, and true to his word we moved our CP, a variant of the AFV432 (Armoured Fighting Vehicle) within the hour.

Some years later, on my second tour of Germany; I joined a group called Arbeitsgemeinschaft für Spechte (Woodpecker Study Group) and attended a conference at Vosswinkle Wildlife Park on woodpeckers in Arnsberg, Nordrhein-Westfalen.

Here, if we were lucky, we could see seven of what was then ten species of woodpecker in Europe; there are now eleven with the Iberian Green Woodpecker being split from the Green; the Grey-headed and Middle-spotted being specialities in that area. During the evening there were several talks, one was on the Middle-spotted, and the person giving the presentation had done his thesis on this woodpecker. During his talk he made many statements, one of which was that of all the spotted woodpeckers in Europe, the Middle-spotted does not regularly drum. Any drumming that is done is mild and limited to early spring; it's usually made in response to competition from another male. Both adults do however tap loudly at the nest-hole. He also stated that the bird never goes down to the ground.

The next day, he led a walk to look for woodpeckers, and at one point we saw a spotted woodpecker fly from the ground up into a tree. We located and identified it as a Middle-spotted and he immediately responded to our cries of the fact that this one was on the ground by saying, "Clearly this bird has not read my thesis". Bless him, Larf (laugh) I near wet myself.

I recently decided that I would have a bucket list; my aim is to see all the distinct species of woodpeckers in the world. Before travelling I often contact local birders for information on the most productive places to bird because local knowledge is worth its weight in gold. They ask me what I would like to see so I tell them my order of priority which is: woodpeckers and owls followed by endemics, and after that everything else is a bonus. One local birder said it really got them to focus their mind on the best places to visit in order to get maximum return. I tend to aim for the rarer woodpeckers, as the more common woodpeckers will be around.

Neuschwanstein Castle is south-east of Füssen in Bavaria where it stands in the shadow of the Tegelberg mountain. If you look down from the mountain when the mist is thick on the ground, the castle looks like it is sitting on a cloud. The Tegelberg is where I learnt to ski with the army, the exercise was called 'Snow Queen'.

News arrived at our CP while we were carrying out a communications exercise, prior to deploying to our annual firing camp in the north of Germany. None of the single men wanted to go on a ten day all-expenses paid skiing trip, during firing camp. They would even get the cost of their food and accommodation back, making a saving of about 50DM (Deutschmarks). I said to my Battery Commander (BC) that I would love to go, the BC responded with "why don't you?" I reminded him that I was married, and that the exercise was aimed at single personnel and we had our annual firing camp coming up. He said, "do you want to go?" I said "yes". He replied "Done, you're on it". While the guys were knee deep in mud in the gun positions, feeling cold, wet and pissed off, I had ten days learning to ski for 150DM. I didn't get a refund for food and accommodation, but I did get to enjoy Bavarian beer and some great birds.

On the first day our instructor took us to the top of the Tegelberg by cable car for a look around. The Tegelberg is in the Ammergau Alps, Füssen and Neuschwanstein Castle are about two kilometres away. While walking around I noticed some wooden ramps hanging over the edge of the mountain. It was a long way down and all I could see were loads of large rocks and treetops. I said, "what mad person would ski off these?". The instructor piped up, "you idiot, they are for the hang-gliders to launch themselves off". Ever felt like an idiot, I did that day. Between Füssen and Oberammergau where the passion play takes place every ten years, I bagged my first White-backed Woodpecker at a place called Linderhof.

I was heading up the slope on the T-bars for a ski run, when I heard one of my buddies calling out to me. He was pointing skywards, looking up I saw my first Golden Eagle gliding across the sky. I was so taken aback that I fell off the T-bar and, in the process, I took out twenty or more skiers coming up behind me. We had only gone about fifty metres up the slope. As the other skiers were piling on top of me, we became a mass of bodies, with skis and sticks jutting out in all directions and I was frantically trying to get them off me, so I could continue to watch the eagle. To say they were not happy with me would be a real understatement.

As we returned to our billets (living quarters), after a good day's skiing, I spotted a Lynx in a field near to our hut. As soon as we stopped, I dropped my kit off, grabbed my bins (binoculars) and headed out to find it. I located its tracks and followed them; this was my first attempt at tracking. As I followed the tracks, I discovered a deer kill; I took pictures and sent them to the National Park telling them of my find. I got a reply, which denied that Lynx occurred in that area. Since then I have found out that a population of five to ten Lynxes had been introduced into the Bohemian-Bavarian forest in the 1970s, later they were supplemented with a further eighteen individuals. On my return from tracking the Lynx I watched an Ermine, (a Stoat), in its white winter coat; playing in the deep snow, running under it and reappearing some distance away, it looked around and then disappeared back under the snow again.

I had fun watching its playfulness as I ate my evening meal. Its pelt was used historically in royal robes in Europe, and the term ermine refers to the animal's white coat.

We would often be deployed on exercise to Eringerfeld, which lay to the north of our camp. It was a nice spring day; I was sitting just inside the edge of a wood enjoying the cool breeze. With our NBC suits on

(Nuclear Biological Chemical), we were waiting for our orders to carry out a section attack on an enemy position, which was in the wood on the other side of a clearing. Great Spotted Woodpeckers were drumming all around us, when I heard them drumming, I felt so relaxed and at ease with the world. Eringerfeld is a great area for birding, with Harriers being the most common bird of prey. Then came the order to mask up and prepare to move. Gas mask on, it was very warm in my NBC suit and when the order came to attack, with my weapon I moved rapidly, zig zagging and screaming as I went.

About halfway across, we had to take cover, I jumped into one of the many large holes that were peppered around the clearing. I was in mid-air when I saw a couple getting it together in the hole that I had chosen to take cover in. Landing on top of the man who was on top of the woman; I could see the horror on the lady's face, her eyes were wide, and she screamed like I had never heard a woman scream before. Meanwhile her man was trying to shake me off his back. As they scrambled to get dressed, some of the other guys followed me into the same crater. The woman was going crazy; her face looked like she had just seen an alien. They were soon up and running away from us, it was all I could do to compose myself; we concluded that they would never do it in nature again.

While serving as a soldier there were countries we were not allowed to go to due to their political climate. After leaving the army these restrictions no longer applied, the leash was gone and off I went. One such country that I visited was the Yemen. While there I hired a lovely man called Yousuf Mohageb as my guide. The first obstacle I had to overcome was on arrival at the airport. Customs wanted to check my bags; on seeing my telescope and bins they became very interested in the nature of my business in their country. Yousuf could see that they were asking me lots of questions and he managed to get to me in the customs area. Quite how he did it I am not sure, but I was glad he did as communication was difficult due to the obvious language risk barrier.

Eventually, they let me go and Yousuf explained what had happened as he quickly rushed me out from the airport. They actually thought that I was some kind of spy! I'd be a very poor one if I was. Yousuf did not want to invite anymore questions, hence beating a hasty retreat from the airport. He said that they found it very strange that someone would want to watch birds. The Arabian Woodpecker was my target bird, it breeds in the montane forests from the south-west of Saudi Arabia to the north-west of Yemen. For as long as I can remember I have wanted to see this woodpecker, and I was not disappointed. I had excellent views of it for three days in a row and not only did I bag a pair of Arabian Woodpeckers on the first day, there was also a Wryneck calling in the background; I love their distinctive call; I could listen to it all day. I even have it as one of my ringtones on my mobile phone: this is so that when I am working in nature with my clients the Wrynecks call blends in better than a typical ringtone does.

During the whole trip we managed to see twelve of the thirteen endemics that occur in the country; the Arabian Wheatear, the Yemen Linnet and the Yemen Serin are among the thirteen. The other obstacle we had to overcome was the abundance of military checkpoints. At one checkpoint I was asked to take my Bergen (backpack) out of the back of the vehicle, stepping out from our vehicle I towered over the guy holding his AK47; he took one look up at me and waved us on. I kind of got the feeling my size put him off checking our vehicle. Bonus.

Many people wonder if Yemen is safe. I guess you need to judge that for yourself. Personally, I found it safe, mainly because Yousuf would not take any risks himself for the sake of his wife and children. He was always very vigilant, taking great care to ensure my safety. The countryside was fantastic, and the people were friendly. They always wanted to know what I was doing; especially the children sometimes I would let them look through my telescope or bins. On one occasion we were having lunch in a local establishment and sitting opposite us on the floor were five men dressed in typical Arabic attire with their AK47s on their laps. They struck up an interesting and diverse conversation with us, I guess they do not come across many westerners and like me, they had enquiring minds. At no point did I feel threatened, in fact quite the opposite. It was a real pleasure to exchange views and not feel judged by the person holding an opposite view. However, while I was there, I always had to pay attention to which hand I used to eat my food with, ensuring I ate using my right hand. On one occasion I was challenged about why I was using my left hand. In Islam it is allowed to use your left hand if your wrist is broken or for some other good reason but otherwise the general rule is that the right hand is intended for noble matters and the left is intended for lowly matters. While it is not prohibited to use the left hand, to do so without a valid need is seen as offensive.

We drove north-west for Kawkaban, a fortified citadel about 2,931 m (9,616 ft.) above sea level. The city was built on a precipitous hilltop walled from the north and fortified naturally from the other directions. Here, we bagged an endemic Philby's Partridge, we also saw Red-capped Larks and Red-breasted Wheatears, both of which were plentiful on the flat open arable land just outside the city wall. At the local reservoir there were a few waders and looking across from the clifftop to the cliff on the opposite side I spotted a Red Fox curled up asleep on a ledge, about thirty feet below the top. From the top of the city there was a line of lush green vegetation running all the way to the bottom for about three or four hundred feet. This made for good birding and as sure as eggs are eggs, I bagged a pair of Arabian Accentors, another endemic to the Yemen.

Its natural habitat is subtropical or tropical high-altitude scrubland; as with many other birds it is threatened by habitat loss. I decided I wanted to sleep out for the night directly below the citadel, we acquired some mattresses from a local café, and set up camp on a dead-end road, with one single streetlamp. I was hoping to see a Hume's Tawny or Desert Owl during this trip. However, I was not expecting to see it fly past us that evening, it stood out in the light from the streetlamp. In the distance behind me I could hear a Little Owl calling from high up on the cliff. The next day we moved onto a Wadi (a dry riverbed) were we birded there for a while. As we were about to leave, the local Bedouin drove up to us. Yousuf stopped me from continuing to bird and asked me to focus on the Chieftain, which makes sense as it would have been rude for me to carry on birding. The Chieftain chatted with Yousuf for a while. Yousuf later told me that he had invited us for a meal, it took great skill on Yousuf's part to get us out of going as it is considered rude not to accept a meal, especially from a Chieftain. During this time, I dipped on what I believed was a Citrine Wagtail, it had taken flight just as Yousuf called me over.

Shortly after this Yousuf and I had the most amazing experience, we were treated to a full-on display from a Long-legged Buzzard, in full summer plumage only seventy-five meters away. This bird put on the most astonishing display I have ever seen from a bird of prey. He swooped, alighting gently on a small branch in a tree without breaking it. Rising on a current of warm air directly above the tree, he spun round several times while diving, in another attempt to grab a branch a second time. Rising again he flipped over, swooping with such ease and skill that any Red Bull Air Race World Champion would have been proud of. The buzzard did this for ten minutes or more, during which you could hear me exclaiming with great excitement that this was out of this world. I had never seen anything like it in my life. Yousuf said "that was meant for us" and my reply was "you better believe it; this was a gift just for us".

Coming to the end of my trip, Yousuf asked what I would like to see on my last day. I was still missing some of the endemics like the Arabian Partridge, Yemen Thrush, Arabian Warbler, and I really wanted to see an Amethyst Starling as my last bird of the trip. We managed to bag all of the birds I was missing as well as a Diederik Cuckoo, and we literally ended our day with an Amethyst Starling at eye level and just a few feet away from my side of the car, both the Cuckoo and Starling had amazing iridescent plumage, when the light catches them just right, it is similar to our very own European Starling (or Euro Star as the Americans call them). If you had seen the colours reflecting off of its plumage, I think you would agree that it was an awesome bird to end a great trip with.

In a remote location within the wild heart of Northumberland's National Park, I was teaching a tracking course in woodland next to Otterburn military ranges, this area is a paradise for moorland birds, like the Black Grouse and Merlin. With so few humans around, these birds tend to flourish; I would venture to suggest it is because the ranges have been on the Ministry of Defence (MOD) books since 1911 and the humans in those parts tend to be mainly soldiers. During the bird language session, I was explaining to my group about the concentric rings that we generate and that these alert the wildlife to our presence long before we see them. To explain this, I shared a story with them about the San Bushman of Namibia. The San told me that when Zana (which means Woodpecker) calls, it is telling them that someone will soon visit. And indeed, each time this happened the San would call out "Sau" while pointing in the direction of the same tree that I saw my first Bearded Woodpecker in and from which it was now calling. Five minutes later someone visited. No sooner had I explained this, I heard a Great-spotted Woodpecker alarming. I turned around to call to the group to pay attention as a Great-spotted flew right past us! Great and Blue Tits, Blackbirds, and Chaffinches were among the other birds that came bursting through the woodland, it appeared they were following the woodpeckers lead on which direction to fly in order to escape the perceived danger. We then scanned the woodland in the direction from which the birds had flown, and sure enough there was a whole bunch of people walking along the boardwalk throwing a concentric-ring and alerting the birds to their presence. Because of the disturbance they were making, the Great-spotted Woodpecker alerted not only us but the other wildlife of the potential danger. The Red Squirrels in turn gave out an alarm call as did other wildlife. I said to my group prior to this incident that I had planned to throw a concentric-ring while they were in their sit-spots, so that they could observe how the birds reacted to my presence in the woods, there was no need to now; nature had taken care of it for me. Over the weekend I watched the Red Squirrels playfully chasing each other in and around the trees, what a joy it was to sit and watch them.

During the weekend, artillery guns were firing, but not as much as we used to when I served in the Gunners. I could hear them firing off to my left, moments later I heard the shells passing overhead as they sliced through the air, and a while later I heard the distinctive crump of the shells exploding in the distance. I relayed this to my friend who was hosting the course; I told him I had not slept so well in years as I did that night. He responded in his lovely Yorkshire accent, "Hey lad, get rid of them Namby-pamby new age CD's you listen to and play some guns firing, maybe you will sleep like a baby from now on".

During my time in Namibia, one of the things I did was build a shelter typical for that environment. I enjoyed building it, as it helped to improve on my skills as a bushcraft instructor. I spent the night in it, with a small fire just inside the entrance, good job too, as quite a few Jackals and Hyenas passed close by the entrance to my shelter. The next day we tracked animals with the San, on one occasion we stalked a herd of Springbok, well the San stalked, we were like a herd of Elephants and I was like a bull in a china shop. The San were remarkably patient with us when we spooked the Springbok. The San are amazing as they moved like the antelope; doubled over, their bodies never moved up or down they were always kept level while their legs were going ten to the dozen.

Dan, my San guide, told me that they (the San) called me 'Sau' which means 'Tree'. I felt that this was a rather appropriate description of me, given that I am a big fella. I also found it interesting, because much of my work as a Nature-based counsellor involves working with people in the woods, with trees and other nations of the natural world. By other nations I mean plants, birds and insects etc. I recently discovered when working with two Rabbis that they along with the Native Americans, refer to the trees as a nation.

Over the years I have been very fortunate to have been involved in various bird projects around the world, and several of these involved woodpeckers. Many years ago, I did a drawing of the Cuban Ivory-billed (which may be extinct now) for my Dutch friend Martjan Lammertink. I had the drawing printed onto leaflets and Martjan distributed them throughout the search area where the Ivorybill was believed to be. Sadly, or luckily, depending on your point of view, he did not find it. Who knows maybe one day it will turn up? Is it a good or bad thing to find such rare birds? As we humans tend to ruin things even with the best will in the world.

Richard, a friend and army buddy told me, that he saw my drawing of the Cuban Ivory-billed on the front of a menu card in a restaurant in

Corfu called, believe it or not Woody's. He said that he tried to borrow a menu card on a permanent basis, so that he could give it to me, but the owner clocked him and kept one eye on him from then on. In the end he was unable to procure it for me. It's a nice compliment that they used my drawing. I think Woody's owes me a couple of meals considering they did not ask if it was ok to use it, maybe I need to go there to **Steak** my claim for a free meal, pun intended, sorry.

One of the things I have noticed about South American woodpeckers is the brightness of their red head plumage. I often wondered why this might be, is it because of the surrounding vegetation that they need to be brighter or is it because of the light in that part of the world reflects the colour red in a different way, or could it be part of attracting a mate? Studies on the Middle-spotted Woodpecker have revealed that woodpeckers in better condition appeared to be expressed by a brighter red cap resulting in more offspring being produced. Perhaps mating with a highly ornamented individual could be an evolutionary step towards mutual sexual selection. In short, the brightness of the cap has the potential to reflect the quality of individual birds.

Once again Martjan went off on his travels, this time to Mexico to look for the world's largest, rarest and possibly extinct Woodpecker. Namely the Imperial Woodpecker, which is 56–60cm (22–23.5in) long and 76 cm (30 in) in wingspan, for this project Martjan asked me to do a single drawing showing all the black and white woodpeckers that occur in Mexico. The reason for a single drawing was that due to seeing the leaflets, many people reported seeing the Cuban Ivory-billed. Although on further investigation it turned out to be a different black and white woodpecker all together. Basically, the locals just reported any black and white bird. This time Martjan wanted to try something different, with the single drawing he could ask questions directly of those who claimed to have seen the Imperial Woodpecker, he could then determine if there was any substance to their claims. Alas this bird was not found either. I would so love to see this bird. This drawing was also used in a book without acknowledging me as the artist.

A few years ago, I went to help Martjan deep in the Argentine jungle with his Helmeted Woodpecker (HEWO) research. Prior to departing, Richard told me about a situation where someone he knows got into difficulty in Argentina. The locals found out that his friend was a serving officer in the British Army, and this caused them to become extremely upset, so much so that Richard's friend had to beat a hasty retreat to the airport and leave the country early.

With this in mind I asked Martjan if he had any Argentinians working with him and he said yes. I asked him not to mention that I served in the British Army, to which he agreed. I said that I would avoid all discussion regarding my time in the military. I have to say that I found it very difficult when sharing stories at night around the campfire not to tell army type stories. However, there was one night I very nearly let the cat out of the bag, Martjan had twigged it as well. Thankfully I stopped myself although I felt sure it would not have been a problem as the guys Martjan had on his team were really cool people. That said, it is better to be safe than sorry and I certainly did not want to cause any problems for Martjan, after all once I left, he would still have to deal with any aftermath that might have happened.

As well as radio tagging and tracking the HEWO we also tagged the Robust Woodpecker (ROWO). We built hides from bamboo which we collected from the surrounding area with our machetes. We set up mist nets which were left closed until we returned a day or two later. Sitting in our hides we waited for the woody's to be drawn in by a playback of their calls and the use of decoys, that Martjan had carved out of wood. Holding onto a line attached to the nets we would drop the nets when the shout went out; thankfully the flies were few, so the wait was not so bad. Then the call went out, we had one in the net! Springing into action the net was dropped, and we burst from our hides to remove the woodpecker as quickly and safely as possible from the net. I felt deeply honoured and privileged to hold both HEWO and ROWO, while we radio tagged them. I can tell you these guys can drive their bills hard into your hands while you are holding them. I had to really suck it up, as to let them go would have been unthinkable. This was one of my best field trips especially when Martjan said it was the largest number of woodpeckers he had caught in one day.

Martjan really knows his woodpeckers and on top of that he has no 'stop' button, where he gets his energy and drive from, I do not know. All I know is that by the end of our last walkout I was hallucinating and stumbling all over the place. The concentric-rings I was pushing out let the wildlife for miles around know that we were there. I must have driven Martjan mad. To give you an idea of the routine, our daily walkouts started hours well before dawn and went hours well past last light. During our drive to the site and back we got to see several mammals, one was the Tayra; in Argentina it is known as the Huron Grande. At first, I thought it was a Black Jaguar then Martjan corrected me. The Tayra is an omnivorous animal from the weasel family, native to the Americas. We saw a juvenile Lesser Anteater, and on our last trip we bagged a Black-and-White Hawk-Eagle as it cruised down the track flying a few feet directly over our vehicle, what an awesome sight that was.

I travelled to Trinidad and Tobago (T&T) for a birding trip over the Christmas period and as per normal I packed my kit into my DPM (Disruptive Pattern Material) Bergen (backpack). DPM is the term used for a camouflage pattern. While waiting for my flight at Heathrow, my intuition was telling me to buy a new backpack and put mine in a locker, at the time I did not act on this and in hindsight I now know why I should have. I checked my Bergen in, boarded my flight, landed and cleared passport control; it was only when I reached customs that it became clear why I should not have travelled to T&T with a DPM Bergen. A customs official proceeded to empty my Bergen out, he picked up my knife, removed it from its sheath looked at it, replaced it back in the sheath and returned it to me. He then confiscated my Bergen stating that I was not allowed to enter the country with it, as it is seen as having the potential for me to commit robbery with it.

When I asked him why he was not taking my knife away from me, he replied that it had a black handle and not a DPM one. He went on to explain that with a DPM item I could hide in the undergrowth, ambush people and then proceed to rob them. I responded with "are you for real?" No amount of persuading could convince him that I needed it in order to move around the country. I ended up entering the country with two black plastic bags which I had in my Bergen to keep my stuff dry. In my humble opinion I would suggest this person was a classic case of SMS – Small Man Syndrome or Stupid Man Syndrome, maybe even both.

He seemed to be getting drunk on his position of power. Even though I was annoyed by him, without him I would not have had some the experiences I encountered in T&T. Fortunately for me I befriended someone on the flight who took pity on me and offered me the opportunity to travel with her to where she was staying. Her driver was a really nice guy and he offered me a backpack to travel with. It was however his daughter's school satchel; it was small and pink and because it was so small, I could not take all of my stuff.

Apu the driver, agreed to look after my tripod and some other bigger items. We arranged to meet up at the airport at the end of my trip to return his daughter's satchel. So, off I went on my birding tour of T&T, all six foot four of me with a girl's pink school satchel on my back. I hitched a lift to Asa Wright, a well-known Bird Sanctuary and one of the few roosts for the Oilbird in Latin America. The Oilbird is found in the northern areas of South America including Trinidad. They nest in colonies within caves, feeding on fruits from the oil palm and tropical laurels. They are the only nocturnal, flying, fruit-eating birds in the world.

Foraging at night, with their specially adapted eyesight, navigating using echolocation in much the same way as bats do, they are one of the few birds to do so. Asa Wright was originally a coffee & cocoa plantation, which now has over 2,000 acres of protected land and it's a great sanctuary for the exotic birds of Trinidad. I was travelling on a shoe-string budget so I could only afford one night at this eco lodge, and in order to see the Oilbird, Asa Wright required that people stayed a minimum of three nights before they would take you to see this stunning bird. Luckily for me, a member of staff was interested in wilderness-living-skills and having found out that I had attended the Tracker school in the States with Tom Brown Jr, we got talking. In exchange for sharing some of my skills and knowledge with him, he arranged for me to hook up with an American group.

The next morning, I had the good fortune to see the Oilbird. They were roosting in a cave at the bottom of a valley with a fast-flowing river running through it. We could only go so far into the cave due to the restrictions placed upon us by the river. However, we got far enough to get excellent views of these fascinating birds sitting on a ledge as the river flowed underneath them. It was truly an amazing sight to see such a rare bird. Afterwards I went birding around the sanctuary, after bagging a White Bellbird I happened upon a large white bell-shaped flower.

The flowers were overhanging the path I was on; I began to wonder which hummingbirds would feed from this flower and as I reached out to touch one, I got a strong sense not to. I had no idea what the flower was called. After returning to the UK, I was at work in a challenging behaviour home. We were watching a programme about buying and selling houses, when I saw the same flower in the garden. I said to the staff that I had just seen that flower in Trinidad, when one of them turned to me and said that it's an Angels' Trumpet, all parts of the plant are poisonous, and you do not want to touch it. I am glad I listened to my intuition not to touch it. The following day I travelled with the Americans I had hooked up with the day before. We went to see the Scarlet Ibis's return from feeding in Venezuela, which is about 11 miles from Caroni Swamp. I ended up on a bus on my own as the other bus was full. On the way the driver and I were chatting, and I told him that my favourite bird was the woodpecker. He said we should do a detour as he had a woodpecker nesting in his garden. "I'm happy with that" I said. It turned out to be a Crimson-crested Woodpecker. I had limited views of the male looking out from the nest hole, this was a great start to the day which soon got even better. We climbed into our boat and pushed off for one of the small islands that the Scarlet Ibises roost on. I made every effort to locate birds in the mangroves as we drifted past, although not many birds made an appearance apart from one Common Potoo, and a Gray-necked Wood Rail. It was almost dusk as we puttered through the eerie lagoons with scattered islands of fifty shades of green. We moored alongside several other boats, now it was just a case of waiting for the arrival of the Ibises. Soon, they started to drift in, at first one or two, then three or more, the numbers slowly built up and then they came in waves. Coming in from all directions were these bright rosy pink birds. I found it very thrilling and as time went on it got better, as hundreds and hundreds of scarlet birds cruised in, to land in one of the tree covered islands. Their vibrant red feathers filled the sky as they returned to the swamp, eventually the trees looked like they were covered in bright crimson flowers. To witness them coming in to roost was a real privilege and should not be missed by anyone, even non-birders.

The people of Tobago are different to those in Trinidad; both are very friendly towards strangers, however in Trinidad people were so laid back they were almost horizontal. They had a way about them that endeared you to them. I felt like I was at home, I could have lived there for sure. I got a taxi from the airport and headed for the far end of the island where I was meeting up with a local bird guide. The cabby recommended a good B&B. I booked in, dumped my kit on the bed and off I went exploring. Sometime later while up a hill just outside the village, I heard a car horn. It sounded like someone was trying to draw attention to themselves, I went to investigate and sure enough that was the case. A dreadlocked man was standing by his car, as I approached, he turned out to be my guide. I asked him how he knew that I was here as I had planned to call him later that day. He said, "man the drums were beating, they said a giant of a man with long hair had just arrived and was asking where he could find me"; he continued "as I searched the village looking for you, people pointed him in the direction of where they had seen me going".

We chatted for a while making our plans for the next few days. I saw no woodpeckers during this period, until I met a German couple who gave me a good tip for a Red-rumped Woodpecker. I hitched a lift to the opposite side of the island; it was late when I arrived and there was just enough time to do a short recce (reconnaissance) before getting my head down. I crashed out for the night on a bench near to the beach. Early the next morning I was up and off looking for the Red-rumped Woodpecker, having searched for the best part of the morning I was having no luck in finding it, I decided it was time to go. I turned around to head back and above me, some twenty meters away was a male Red-rumped Woodpecker feeding. In my head I said the words 'in the bag'. This is a phrase that I picked up from my German friends, when we went trapping and ringing birds. After catching a bird, we would put it into a cloth bag and take it back to our ringing station. I adopted it and would call it out when I saw a new species of bird. The German for in the bag is 'In der Beutel'.

It was now time to head back to Trinidad, but first I needed to go to the bank as it was coming up to Christmas day and I needed some money. I was shocked to discover that, had I changed my pounds directly into TT (Trinidad & Tobago Dollars) I would have doubled my spending power, as opposed to changing my pounds into US dollars and then into TT, this was a lesson learnt. I said to myself "note to Geoff, do more research before travelling". On entering Trinidad, I was stopped by a very big lady in uniform. With my arms outstretched, she patted me down, asking me what I was doing in Tobago; she then felt something lumpy in my right trouser leg pocket; she said, "what is in here". I replied, "oh that, that's my VIP", her colleagues were sitting nearby looking puzzled. She leaned back, one hand on her hip, and looking me in the eye she retorted "are you some kind of diplomat" at the same time I reached into my pocket and pulled out the item in question. I responded with "no, it's my **V**ery **I**mportant **P**aper," as I showed her my flattened toilet roll. At which point she clipped me on the arm and told me to move on, her colleagues however, were literally falling off their chairs in tears of laughter. I can see them now in the pub telling their friends and having a good laugh about it.

Eventually the time came to leave the country all together and return home; I made one more attempt at retrieving my Bergen but to no avail. I met with the manager of customs, and low and behold the customs official who I referred to as SMS turned up as well. I said to the manager in the interests of health and safety tell him to leave the room. He kept interrupting me, to the point where I was not willing to let him do that anymore. His boss told him to leave. However, my journey was not yet over.

As arranged, Apu the guy who lent me his daughter's pink satchel arrived to collect it and to return my stuff. I was already in the line-up for check in, so we swapped our stuff, I thanked him for his kind support in my hour of need and off he went. I checked in, as I cleared passport control, I sensed that I was going to be stopped for a random drugs test and sure enough I was stopped. The officer said that they had been informed by someone that I was carrying drugs and asked if I would agree to a swab test. I agreed, I thought they either saw the exchange at check-in or it was a standard line they used to see how someone would react to being told that someone had reported them.

Even though you know you are not guilty your mouth still dries up and your capacity to speak becomes difficult. After being asked lots of questions, a very large official, bigger than me arrived and began giving me the third degree. It appeared that they did not believe my story as to why I was in their country. This went on for a long time and it got to a point where I felt I needed to change the situation. I said to the official, "would you rather that I lied to you?" he looked puzzled, I went on to say "well you do not seem to want to believe the truth so maybe if I lied that would be better". He looked me in the eye and said, "RESPECT, okay you may go". As I walked away, I said to myself "whatever you do Geoffrey, do not look back, you may turn into a pillar of salt". Thankfully the trip home was uneventful.

I stayed for one night in Bangkok, Thailand. During this time, I witnessed a street fight, kick boxing style. It was interesting to watch, however I stayed in the background not wishing to be sucked into it, should it get more explosive than it already was. That night, I hired a guy with his 4x4 to take me to Khao Yai National Park the following morning; the park is on the western side of the San Kamphaeng Mountain Range. Khao Yai is the third largest park in Thailand, covering an area of 300 square kilometres, ranging from tropical forests to grasslands. The park boasts some 320 species of birds and has an elevation range from 400–1,000 m. I based myself in lodgings at the entrance to the park for a week and each day I walked into the park, sometimes hitching a lift to the information centre. I tended to stick to the main tracks however on my way back one day I went off the main road and up into the hills. I passed a herd of Indian Elephants that were grazing in a clearing. They were around 1km away so I posed no threat to them, not that I would contemplate taking on an elephant.

I made my way along a track stopping now and then, when a Heart-spotted Woodpecker alighted on a tree close to me. Seconds later it was off, it appeared to be on a mission, as it was zigzagging its way through the jungle from tree to tree. I continued my walk when I heard a tapping sound. I left the track making sure that after a short distance I turned around to view the forest from the direction I would be returning from. I followed the tapping until I came across a Common Flame-backed Woodpecker. I watched it working its way in and around a large tree stump. I tried tapping a stick against a tree to see if I could draw it closer to me. It paid no attention to my tapping as it seemed more focused on foraging, or maybe it did not recognise the tapping sound I was making, which our Great-spotted responds to. The time came to move on, I followed my tracks back onto the trail; checking for snakes or any other unwelcomed surprises along the way. As I stepped onto the main track, I came face to face with a Dhole (a wild dog) it was coming up the trail towards me; it was completely unaware of my presence until I was about three metres away.

The Dhole was startled to see me standing there, it gave a short single growl and then proceeded to walk around me just inches from my leg, it then carried on up the trail without looking back. To see the Dhole so close to me, caused me to shift from a relaxed state to a state of alertness, this change in my energy was when the Dhole became aware of my presence. It was an amazing experience to be so close to a wild dog.

As a young lad in boarding school I would often look through a book on the birds of the world and the Sultan Tit was one bird that always stood out from the pages, along with the Arabian Woodpecker. My wish then was to see the Sultan Tit and that wish came true as I walked down a trail, a flock of them passed me by. What a cracking bird. On my way back to the information centre, I came across a Blue Pitta, it was getting dark, so I decided to track it down the next day.

The following morning, I set out to see if I could find it, eventually I spotted it, it had seen me coming before I saw it. It was watching me from the end of a trail; then, when it decided I was close enough it ran off down the trail. I decided to stalked slowly up to a tree on the bend using it to screen myself from the Pitta in the hope of getting a better view, as I looked from behind the tree, there it was, waiting for me at the next bend, some thirty meters away. Just as I showed my face, it ran off again. This was repeated several times and always it was waiting for me at the next bend. I found it very amusing indeed and I had fun playing this game with him, tough I am sure for the Pitta it was not a game or WAS IT? I suspect it was leading me away from its nest, because it eventually flew off passing me as it returned close to where I first saw it. My trip was now at an end and I decided to catch the train back to Bangkok, on route I had some great views of Storks, waders and many other birds sitting on the wires along the railway track. The train took me straight into the airport and after checking in I decided to a grab a bite to eat, I saw a slice of cheesecake which I really fancied and THEN I saw the price. Here's the thing, to hire a guy and his 4x4 for the day to take me to Khao Yai cost 1500 Baht, my return on the train cost 80 Baht, but the slice of cheesecake would have cost me 3000 Baht. Go figure, it was cheaper to hire a driver and his truck for the day than it was to buy a slice of cheesecake at the airport. I met a very interesting American in the airport lounge, we struck up a conversation; we chatted about all sorts of things, politics being one of the topics. He said something that I found very amusing, which was that the US Congress is the largest collective of non-convicted criminals in the world.

Some years later I returned to Thailand, this time I was there to see my friend Maurice who is an old army buddy. He had settled just outside Khon Kaen running a general store with his wife Dang, I took to calling it 'Open all hours Thai Style'. Maurice Newell is my hero, I mean a real hero, by the true definition of the word and not in the way it gets bandied around today. During his service in Bosnia he helped raise funds to rebuild a Muslim hospital in Sarajevo, he got twenty-six children over to Europe for hospital treatment six of which came to the UK. He raised thousands of pounds and he had toys and other gifts sent out to the children there and like a true hero he sought no credit.

It was great seeing my friend again after so many years, and yet it seemed like it was yesterday that we last met. We talked a lot, putting the world to rights as you do. Their shop is in a village called Ban Dang some 30 km from Khon Kaen; the surrounding area is made up of paddyfields with small scattered woodlands and a river. I bagged Barred Buttonquails and Asian barred-Owlets of which I found three in a small wooded area which surrounded a shrine by the side of the road.

In a bush on the edge of the shrine was a very active and delightful male Scarlet-backed Flowerpecker. The male has navy blue upperparts with a bright red streak running from its crown to its tail coverts, and whitish underparts. I watched him flit around for quite a while. This little bird was quite mesmerising. I could have pulled up a chair and watched him for hours. I searched the paddyfields for birds, in the distance I noticed movement on the edge of a small woodland. This movement turned into a Fulvous Woodpecker which was searching in and around the branches of the trees, looking for grubs and whatever else it could find to eat.

After spending 3-4 days with Maurice it was time to head out. I took the bus from Khon Kaen to Nam Nao National Park. The park covers an area of about 966 square kilometres in the Phetchabun and Chaiyaphum provinces of northeast Thailand. Nam Nao consists mainly of dry, deciduous and pine forests with open areas, lush with grasses, which allowed for some good un-obscured views of the birds in that area. When I arrived at the gatehouse, I paid the entrance fee of 200 Baht (£3.10) and rather than hitch a ride with the rangers I decided to walk the 2 km's to the main building. Birding along the way, bagging some good birds in the process; namely; Velvet Fronted Nuthatch, Grey-capped Pygmy Woodpecker, and a Black Baza. Arriving at the centre, the staff were very friendly and interested in what I was doing. The lodges were in very good order although I was not keen on the squat style toilets. The next day I decided to take one of the longer trails to see if I could find the elephants that were reported to be in the area, and I was told by the rangers that there was also a Tiger around.

As I traversed a large clearing, I encountered lots of Crested Treeswift's; these delightful little birds were sitting high up on a branch of a large tree which was located in the centre of the clearing. The Treeswift is a large slender bird measuring 23 cm (9 in) in length, its grey above and white below with long sweptback wings which are a darker grey. Its crest rises up from its upper mandible and it has a long, forked tail. The adult male has orange sides to its face. This cracking bird glues its tiny nest to a branch, which is so small that incubating birds perch upright on the edge of the nest.

After spending some time watching them and other birds, I decided to head for some high ground that bordered a tree line in the distance. As I moved along the trail, towards the ridgeline I had an image pop into my head of a tiger walking along the trail towards me. I wondered if this meant that a tiger had passed down this very trail some hours earlier, or maybe I sensed the presence of a tiger coming my way or was it just plain old wishful thinking? Either way I felt very excited by the prospect of seeing both elephants and a tiger.

As I approached the high ground, a flock of Jays started to create a commotion, causing me to stop at the ridgeline. I was very aware that they were warning of some kind of danger up ahead, perhaps they had discovered an owl, maybe even the tiger or some other dangerous creature. Crouching down, I took in the scene, aware that I might get to see something special. I looked down the trail which led down into dense undergrowth that had large stands of Bamboo scattered throughout the forest. As I waited, I heard an almighty crash; my heart missed a few beats.

My immediate thought was the sound had been made by an elephant crashing through the undergrowth. I waited to see if one would appear, but nothing came. I then began to think it was the tiger charging through the undergrowth after a deer, my heart raced even more. I wondered what would I do if I came face to face with a tiger? After the crash, the Jays settled down and it all went quiet, at which point I felt it was ok to cautiously move forward and investigate what had caused the noise. Moving slowly, I eventually came across a large branch that had broken off of a nearby tree. The branch was some twenty metres long by about one and half metres thick, it was lying on top of a large clump of bamboo. The tree it fell from was massive to say the least, in fact, the branch could have been a tree in its own right, certainly by our standards. I realised that had the Jays not kicked off when they did, then in the time it would have taken me to walk from the ridgeline to that very spot I would have been underneath it, or certainly very close to where it came crashing down. My target bird that day was the Bamboo Woodpecker, which believe it or not frequents Bamboo. Understanding the language of the Jays potentially saved me from either serious injury or even death.

The following day I encountered a White-bellied Woodpecker in the evergreen part of the park. There are some fourteen subspecies of this woodpecker, including the Andaman Woodpecker which is among the largest of the Asiatic Woodpeckers. I was wandering around at dusk, when I saw a large squirrel climbing a tree, as I watched it, it jumped off the tree, it was a flying squirrel, it cruised some twenty feet over my head and landed a short distance away near the base of another tree, it then climbed again, when it reached the height it needed to, it jumped again. I continued to watch it until it was out of sight. Some of the other woodpeckers seen on this trip were the Grey-headed, Lesser and Greater Yellow-naped. In the woodpecker family I also saw Blue-throated, Great, and Coppersmith Barbets.

In terms of woodpecker lifers, (by lifers, I mean birds that I have never seen before) I have to say that to date, my time in and around Seattle wins hands down. I went birding there for two days with Rachel who I had met through a birding website. Rachel was a great host; she asked me what I wanted to see and of course I said woodpeckers. She confessed that she enjoyed the challenge of finding and bagging all the woodpeckers in her area. My target bird was the White-headed Woodpecker, which is a non-migratory bird whose range stretches from the mountains of British Columbia through to southern California. In the southern part of the range the White-headed has a longer bill – especially the males. Apparently, the bill of the southern subspecies is an adaptation for being better able to feed on the large, spiny cones of the Coulter Pines.

We visited a homestead where we spent a good hour or two watching the birdfeeder in the garden of our hosts who said that White-headed Woodpeckers regularly feed at their bird table. Guess what, we didn't see them. We had to move on to the next place which was further to the north up into the High Cascades. While driving up the mountain road I spotted a Townsend's Solitaire, which is a medium-sized thrush, and the only solitaire native to North America. It was flying back and forth along a branch that overhung the road which had caught my attention. We stopped the car and got out to watch it, and after a short while it flew off. I decided to walk up the road for a bit to see what else I could find. As I looked out over the narrow-forested valley, I spotted movement in a tree not too far away. I brought my bins up and low and behold there it was; my first ever White-headed Woodpecker. I jumped for joy, my friend was very pleased that I had found it in the wild and not on a bird table; I had to agree with her. In less than a forty-eight-hour period we saw ten species; six being lifers namely, the Red-breasted, Red-naped and Williamson Sapsucker's, Three-toed, Lewis's and of course White-headed. In my mind no photo, drawing or painting can really do true justice to the Lewis's Woodpecker, you have to see it to believe it. After seeing the Lewis's Woodpecker at an old army base, we returned home, passing by a well-known mountain from a TV series called 'Twin Peaks'. Rachel dropped me off at my friend's place where I was staying. We later met up again independently from each other during a birding trip to Mexico.

My first organised group trip was to Morocco with the Army Ornithological Society (AOS), I thought it would be interesting to see how different it would be from travelling on my own. Morocco was awesome and our guide ran out of birds to show us. One of the most amazing birds we saw was an Egyptian Nightjar a shapeshifter if ever there was one. Its cryptic plumage is much paler than the European Nightjar; the adult is sand-coloured, with buff and brown bars and streaks. The underparts are sandy to whitish, and the male has tiny white wing spots. The camouflage on this bird was out of this world. It had settled in open ground after taking flight and unless you saw where it landed which I had not, you would be hard pushed to locate it. I ended up seeing it through someone else's scope. I observed the tiniest of movement of its head as it watched Tim Cowley, trying to get closer for a close-up photo. It was just so amazing to watch, what a thrill. Some of the other birds we saw were Pharaohs Eagle Owl, Botts Wheatear, Moussier's Redstart, Desert Sparrow and Desert Warbler. A few days later, we were on a beach watching the critically endangered Northern Bald Ibis which is a breeding endemic. A group of these birds landed on the stone beach thirty metres away, they were awesome.

As we drove over the mountains my target bird came within reach, on the last day of all things, and of course the guys upped the pressure, telling me that I would dip on it. "Not so" I said. In the end I bagged two Levaillant's Green Woodpeckers in two different locations, it was well worth the wait even if I was sweating a bit on the possibility that I might dip out on it. But I kept the faith.

My second group trip was to Mexico. After a long and very eventful trip with Michael Carmody of Legacy Tours, (other tour operators are available) our American guide, I bagged the following endemics; Gray-breasted, Golden-cheeked, Gray-crowned, and Strickland's. The other lifers were the Ladder-backed, and Golden-fronted, the non-lifers were the Smoky-brown, Hairy and Pale-billed Woodpeckers. We arrived where the Strickland's Woodpecker was to be found. As we walked the trail it was not long before I bagged my first Red-shafted Flicker.

The red showed up well on the underwing when it took flight. We were about to give up and move to another area when I heard a woodpecker like call coming from behind. Looking up as I turned, I clocked a woodpecker coming in high over the tree canopy in the distance, and it was heading in our direction. It alighted in a large tree closest to me, I put my bins up, I focused and there it was, a magnificent male Strickland's Woodpecker and a few moments later it was joined by a female. Another long-awaited bird now in the bag.

During the trip we saw some excellent birds like the Bee Hummingbird, Transvolcanic Jay, San Blas Jay (both endemics) plus the White-throated Jay and White-throated Magpie-Jay. We left this mountainous area and made our way down to an area of reedbeds, to look for the Aztec Rail a rarity indeed. I was chatting with Cupcake, an American guy who I befriended during our trip. Michael our guide was with an English guy who came solely to find this one bird, this guy was on a mission with a lifer total of 9000 plus birds. They were some distance from us but not too far away that we could not hear the conversation, this was when I introduced Cupcake to the expression 'stringing'. "What's stringing Irish"? Irish was his nickname for me, I explained that stringing is turning a Clapper Rail into an Aztec Rail, (or if you like, turning a Mini Cooper into a London Bus). It's when you want to see a bird so much that you end up convincing yourself that, that is what you saw. Cupcake listened some more and agreed that there was some serious stringing going on from the English guy. Still, I thought if he was happy, that's all that mattered. A year later, I confirmed with Michael at the British Bird Fair that they had not seen it.

In Japan, Lynn (a member of the AOS) and I waited for the typhoon to abate, it gave us time to look through our field guides prior to boarding our plane. We were heading for the Island of Amami, which is part of the Ryukyu Islands. Kaz our guide was a great person to be with, he always went that extra mile for us, and we were never disappointed. Thanks to him we had the most amazing close up encounter with an Amami Woodpecker. It was literally within three arm lengths from me; I was so excited by this encounter that I forgot to take any pictures. This woodpecker is confined to the mature evergreen broadleaf forest in the hills of the island and it was previously considered conspecific (belonging to the same species) with the white-backed woodpecker. I cannot tell you how thrilling it was to be so close to this cracking woodpecker. We bumped into one of the park wardens who showed us a juvenile Pygmy Woodpecker he had in a cardboard box; it had fallen out of its nest hole.

This small island is home to the endemic Amami Woodcock which is considered vulnerable. We spotted quite a few of them as we drove at night along a road. At one point we had what appeared to be a very large Woodcock, until we realised it was an adult with two young tucked under its wing. The young were looking back at us, their eyes lit up by our headlights. Then there were the Amami Rabbits we encountered along the same road; they are often referred to as living fossils because the species is a living remnant of the ancient rabbits that inhabited the Asian mainland. They have since become endangered and survive only on two small islands.

The Okinawan Woodpecker is a critically endangered endemic on the island of Okinawa, which is where we headed to next. Kaz was worried that we might not get to see it. That was until we saw two individuals, who were possibly a breeding pair, fly across the road in front of our car just before we arrived at our hotel. Kaz stopped the car, and we debussed (alighted) and jumped for joy as we bagged this awesome bird. At this point we laughed as we heard Kaz breathing a big sigh of relief. Out of the so called 20-200 remaining birds on the Island we saw fifteen individual birds and heard two, one was calling and the other drumming. We bagged them all over a two-day period, in real time it was less than twenty-four hours. One of our sightings was an active nest located by the side of a fairly busy road. The adults were regularly flying to and from the nest hole, as they fed their young. Lynn managed to film them near to the nest.

You could not have wished for a better sighting, that was for sure. According to Kaz this was the most he had ever seen of this woodpecker in all of his trips to Okinawa. He said, if he was lucky, he might see one individual. It was definitely a bonanza visit. Kaz also said that as far as he is concerned, the Okinawa Woodpecker is a hard bird to see, as there are only a few hundred birds remaining.

Kaz spared no effort in getting us to our target birds. The next morning after leaving our hotel and as far as I could tell, we were the only guests there; we were heading out for our next target the Okinawan Rail. We had travelled a few kilometres from the hotel when we encountered the first Rail. It was running through a rain trench at the side of the road, probing the debris from the last storm looking for its prey. Eventually it found a meaty looking worm it ran past our car, with the worm in its beak, presumably for its young; it was also colour ringed; the rail not the worm. That day we saw eleven of the endangered Okinawa Rails.

Back on the mainland we headed for one of the big parks where we bagged the Azure-winged Magpie another one of our target birds. This species occurs over a large region of eastern Asia. It was thought to be conspecific with the Iberian Azure-winged Magpie, but it seems that recent genetic analysis has shown them to be a distinct species, and yet they look identical, the two populations are separated by 5400 miles (9,000 km). Could this be a case of convergent evolution? Convergent evolution can be seen as similar to parallel evolution, this is when two species independent of each other evolve in the same direction and independently acquire similar characteristics; as is the case with the New and Old-World Vultures. The new world vultures are more closely related to Storks. Next we went on to Mount Fuji which is an active volcano about one hundred kilometres southwest of Tokyo. It is the country's tallest peak, at three thousand seven hundred and seventy-six metres. It is one of Japan's three sacred mountains. We stopped about halfway up the mountain, spending time searching for more birds, when a Japanese Green Woodpecker, another endemic, loomed into view. We parked up and walked up to the foot of Mount Fuji, birding as we went, we were looking for the Japanese Accentor. Then came the call of nature, so I went around to the back of the tourist centre to use what can only be described as the smallest loo in the world. It was so small that I had to squeeze in by walking backwards, and leaving was more risky as the loo was on top of a steep slope, if I had built up too much momentum I could have ended up at the bottom of the slope, and there was no telling how far away that was, as I could not see the bottom; there really was no room for error.

Later we saw another Japanese Green Woodpecker further down the mountain in one of the local parks, where we also encountered a small group of Inoshishi which are also known as Japanese Wild Boar. They ran across the track in front of us, they appeared to be in a hurry, thank goodness. This may be because hunters have apparently been tasked to kill radioactive boars, quite how you can tell a radioactive boar from a non-radioactive boar I have no idea, perhaps the active one glows in the dark. It seems that some were contaminated by the Fukushima nuclear disaster and by all accounts they are breeding uncontrollably and eating toxic nuclear-contaminated food from around the accident site. During this trip we encountered and bagged four of the nine subspecies of the Japanese Pygmy Woodpecker. The next day we went looking for the Brown Dipper.

We encountered a Black Kite as we crossed a bridge, it was flying low; I thought I would see if it would catch some food from me. I threw a piece of meat into the air as it was passing overhead, and sure enough it turned; swooped and grabbed the food mid-air, I threw more food and several catches later we moved on, its flying skill was awesome. We also bagged a Japanese Wagtail on the railings of the bridge. The next day we went looking for the Japanese Green Pigeon, which really is a cool bird, as it likes to drink seawater. We went very early in the morning; when we got there, we settled in and waited for them to arrive. Eventually, twenty plus birds turned up and got straight into drinking and collecting the seawater presumably for their young. No one knows why they drink seawater; it might be related to a deficiency in their diet, possibly minerals that they can only get from seawater. Out of the 300 plus species of pigeon in the world, only the Japanese Green Pigeon has been known to drink seawater. However, recent studies seem to indicate that the Black Wood and the European Wood Pigeons share this remarkable behaviour? Eventually, they took flight and headed for the Tanzawa mountains, where they live and breed in the beech forests there. The Tanzawa mountains are 20-30 kilometres from Terugasaki Beach where we saw them. These birds risk their lives drinking seawater, some of them have been killed by the crashing waves.

The Ivory-billed Woodpecker is one of the largest woodpeckers in the world, at roughly 20 inches (51 cm) long and 30 inches (76 cm) in wingspan. It is native to the virgin forests of South-eastern United States along with a separate subspecies native to Cuba. Because of habitat destruction and, to a lesser extent hunting, its numbers have dwindled to the point where it is uncertain whether any remain. Though reports have indicated it has been seen again within the current century.

It seems that almost no forests today can maintain an Ivory-billed population; I guess that remains to be seen. I recently had the privilege of joining a group searching for the Ivory-billed Woodpecker (IBWP). While looking for the IBWP I got to see the Red-headed Woodpecker and my woodpecker life list increased by one, I was a happy teddy bear.

I was on a marathon trip from the USA to Brazil but prior to dropping down into Brazil I went to stay with Phillip Knights an army buddy who settled with his good lady Jennifer in Georgia. Phil, who is not a birder, had arranged access onto a military training area for me. An area where some four hundred clusters of the endangered Red-cockaded Woodpecker occur. A cluster consists of at least one male and female and a helper from the previous brood. The area we were given to search by a member of the conservation team within the military base was close to where Phil lived. The next morning, we were out looking for it and it was not long before we heard it drumming. It seemed like it was a long way off in the distance that was until I entered the forest from the track and found myself stood right underneath it. It was a privilege to see this ventriloquist of the woodpecker world; my excitement was matched by its rarity. I called Phil over to see it; when we returned to the truck, Phil said he felt excited by the experience. I said to him after all our years in the army, trying to get the guys into birdwatching it had finally worked, some twenty odd years later. Phil said that he was excited by my excitement from seeing it.

It was now time to head for Brazil my target bird, the Kaempfer's Woodpecker, considered a subspecies of the Rufous-headed Woodpecker. However, in 2003 the South American Classification Committee recognised it as a distinct species. This was based on the differences in habitat, size and plumage, combined with the large distance of more than 3000 kilometres [1850 miles] between the ranges of the two species.

Kaempfer's Woodpecker is strongly associated with Guadua Bamboo and specialises in feeding on the ants found inside the bamboo canes. It can be found across a large portion of Brazil's Cerrado (tropical savannah) region and its habitat is being increasingly fragmented by agricultural activities such as the planting of soy, infrastructure development, and land-clearing for ranching. Sadly, it does not occur in any protected areas, in addition, no stronghold site or concentration of this bird has been identified, thus it is at risk of imminent of extinction.

I started this chapter with the Green Woodpecker so it is only fitting that I should end it with what is known as a Split. As I said earlier the Iberian Green Woodpecker was split from the European Green Woodpecker. Some may consider this an advantage because their life list is increased by one. That is all well and good until you lose a woodpecker/ bird off your list due to Lumping. In my case I had the Campo and Field Flickers on my list, but they have now been lumped together, so I lose one. In the case of the Green Woodpecker my European list was complete until the split. It is now complete again having bagged the Iberian Green in Madrid. I wonder what other surprises await me around the corner.

CHAPTER 2

Owls

As night falls, the moon begins to cast its shadows throughout the land; I am sitting here in the cool night air with a light breeze passing over my face. In the distance the mist is gathering and soon I will need to depend on my hearing alone. What was that? I turn; something is slipping through the trees. My eyes adjust quickly, and I relax. It's just a fox weaving its way through the forest, he appears to be wandering around, checking things out, I guess. Suddenly, I am joined by my partner, "you made me jump. I did not hear you coming". Once again, my attention is drawn to the surrounding area. I am looking for something to hunt down, I am hungry and in need of food. I decide to move on, silently and with stealth I move through the forest and then out into the open fields, hugging close to the edges of wood line to see what turns up.

I have all the tools I need to help me hunt. I have learnt that even with my eyes closed, if I tune into my surroundings I can still hunt. My hearing and awareness are at one with the natural world; it's been several hours now, and I've not had any luck with the hunt. I think I will rest until dawn and then go for one more attempt at finding food. Dawn is not far off now; I know this because I can hear my friends calling in the distance. As I start out to join them, I am presented with an opportunity to make a kill, I turn, and I pounce. Success, with my tummy full I head for the trees for protection and for another rest. Who am I? Why, I am just your regular Tawny Owl of course.

Next to woodpeckers, owls are one of favourite birds and while living in Germany I had the opportunity to experience many owls up close. There were a few times when I had egg on my face due to my lack of identification skills or to be more precise my listening skills. I was asked by my German friends, Wolf and Andreas, to map the location of Little Owls in my area. This was my first attempt at mapping. I went out between the hours of Nineteen hundred (7pm) and Midnight. I found it easy to locate the little ones; as I could hear their calls everywhere. I duly plotted them on my map by locating where their calls were coming from. I was made up; I believed I had done a cracking job. When I reported the large number of owls I had heard (50+) to Wolf and Andreas they questioned it. The next night we went out to the first place that I had marked on my map. They listened and then they smiled, as they both looked at me, they informed me that the Little Owls, I had heard were in fact Lapwings. How embarrassing. After that experience you would have thought that I had learnt my lesson. I was in

Eringerfeld one of my local areas, I was looking for a Wryneck which was reported to be in the area. Eringerfeld, was also the area where we were deployed for 'Exercise Active Edge'; this is a periodical readiness exercise used to practice the call out of the whole of BAOR (British Army of the Rhine) in the event of a World War, and in response to the Warsaw Pact steam rolling over the border.

The Wryneck is so called due to its behaviour of twisting its neck from side to side. With its cryptic plumage it gives the appearance of being snake like, and in so doing probably wards off any threats to its life. It did not take long to locate it, this was due to its distinctive call; nearby I also heard the call of a Scops Owl, which well was out of its range.

It was now late afternoon as I rushed to the nearest phone box located in Geseke, which was about three kilometres away (we didn't have mobiles back then). I called Karl a friend of mine who lived close by, I told him to get out here quickly, informing him that I had a Scops Owl. While I waited for him to arrive, I tried to find the owl, which was proving very difficult. Eventually Karl and Wolf turned up and by now it was dusk. As we stood and listened, it called again. They both reacted in the same way that I did, that was until another call was heard, and then another and another and yet another. We followed the sound of one of the calls. Karl turned over a stone and there looking up at us was a Midwife Toad, with its yellow underbelly, doing a good rendition of a Scops call. I did not feel as embarrassed as last time, as my friends also thought it was a Scops Owl. On the plus side though, I did get great views of the Wryneck. On another occasion my friends and I were birding in the Teutoburger Wald. This is a range of forested hills in the German states of Lower Saxony and North Rhine-Westphalia. After a good day's birding we were walking back to the car when David said that he often sees a Wryneck in this area. In that moment we spotted a bird sitting in the middle of the road. We all stopped, lifted our bins to our eyes and sure enough there it was, a Wryneck. Suddenly, Richard called out the name of a bird I had been trying to see for years, that elusive bird, the one I was always dipping on (dipping meaning, missed out on, did not see). I looked up to see that it was entering the tree line on the far side of a clearing. Once again, this bird eluded me, and my friends had a good laugh at my expense. I would suggest that most birders have at least one bird that they just cannot bag.

One day we were trapping and ringing Little Owls, Wolf had his arm down a hole in a Willow Tree, to see if any owls were present, suddenly he gave a startled cry. We turned to see a Weasel running up his arm and over his shoulder, jumping off him it legged it along the hedgerow until it was out of sight.

If that was not enough, sometime later in the same area with a different tree, he encountered Hornets in the hole, at which point we all legged it. Little owls are quite funny, when you try to get them out of their hole, they dig in hard. Their legs and talons are braced against the wall of the hole, their wings are out and tight against the walls and sometimes they even used their beaks to stop you getting them out of the hole, who could blame them? There is a method in getting them out without causing them harm, although stress is a factor we considered, so we kept our time with them to the bare minimum.

I have ringed many birds; the Spotted Flycatcher, Barn Swallow, and Sand Martin, to name a few. I have also trapped and ringed Tengmalm's Owl, also known as the Boreal owl. In the Arnsberger Wald (Wald meaning Forest), we only had six breeding pairs; it was a rare bird indeed. The location we worked in was a short distance from the Möhnesee Dam, which was one of three dams that was targeted by the famous 617 Dam Buster Squadron in WWII. I remember a friend of mine Alan Warburton telling me that he took his family on a day trip to the Möhnesee Dam. He said that he'd had trouble finding it and decided to ask an old German guy for directions. In those days our car licence plates were very distinctive, until the IRA started hitting us in Germany at which point, we switched to German style plates. Pulling over, he asked for directions and the old guy whilst noting the number plate said (in German), "Englander?" (English). Alan replied "yes", to which the old man said, "you found the Dam forty years ago, go and find it again" or words to that effect.

While checking one of the nest boxes that the owls used, we discovered a Short-toed Treecreeper nest wedged between the box and the tree; what a clever tactic, it had its own personal bodyguard so to speak. I am not so sure if there was any benefit for the owl within that relationship though.

I served in several regiments within the Royal Artillery (RA). In one regiment we had a Colonel (CO) who, in my experience, didn't speak to soldiers below the rank of sergeant; except to issue orders. He kept a Filofax, and in this he would record information such as the interests of every Soldier in the regiment from Sergeant and above. I was his driver on exercise and he rarely spoke to me. One day I was called to the Battery Sergeant Major's (BSM) office. The BSM Graham Stacey informed me that the CO wanted all soldiers who were active in their hobbies to put on a display for the Commander of the Royal Artillery (CRA held the rank of Brigadier).

My display was on a birding and a conservation project I was working on at a local gravel pit called the Zachariassee (Zach). Usually, when a display is presented to a visiting dignitary, the CO would carry out an inspection of the display the day before to make sure that everything is as he would like it to be for the visit. On arriving at my stand, the CO asked me to talk him through my display, I did this, and afterwards, as he walked away, he said "well, you are not going to get many people joining your club are you". Startled, I looked at the BSM and asked him what he meant by that comment.

The BSM said he would tell me later, I said, I wanted to know now. He replied, the Colonel wants those with hobbies to come into camp on a weekend and encourage the guys to take part in their interests by taking them out with them. I looked at him and said, "is he mad?". The BSM asked "What do you mean?" I replied, "do you really think that I am going come into camp on a Saturday morning after the lads have been on the lash (drinking) the night before, down the Gas Light (and various other bars that squaddies like to frequent) and say, "right then who is for a bit of birdwatching?". They will F%@king lynch me. It is not going to happen, Sir".

He walked away laughing, because he knew it to be true and the CO was also right in his assessment. There was no way any of the guys would choose to join me on a birding trip, at least not that they would like to admit to. The following day, we were all in the main hall of the cookhouse waiting for the CRA to arrive. The Brigadier turned up and began visiting the displays which ranged from golf, football and of course birdwatching. Eventually the CRA came to me and as he looked at the photographs that I had pinned around a map of Kreis Soest (Kreis means County) on my display board, he asked "what bird is that?" I replied, "It's a Tengmalm's Owl, Sir". The Brigadier informed me that he had never seen one of them before, and he wanted to know what the chances of seeing one were. I thought, clearly, I have a birder on my hands. I said that I would need to check with my German friends as they hold the permits for ringing this owl, but I did not see a problem. I asked him how I could get in touch with him, at which point the CO stepped in and said, "come and see me Bombardier (Corporal)".

That night I spoke with Wolf and Andreas and they agreed to let the CRA come along on our next field trip. The next day, which was a Thursday, I made my way to the Adjutant's office. I knocked on his door and requested to see the CO; he said the CO will not want to be disturbed. I informed him that I was here at the CO's invitation in response to the CRA's request. He got up from behind his desk and knocked on the CO's door (it's amazing what happens when you name drop). As I stood in the doorway of the CO's office, I informed him that I had arranged for the CRA to see the owl on Friday night. While picking up the phone to call the CRA, the CO told me that the CRA is a busy man and he did not think he would go with me at such short notice. At which point I thought, if he is half the birder that I think he is, he will drop everything and come. This is how the phone conversation went: "Hello Sir, its Colonel X here. I have Bombardier McMullan with me. He says he has arranged for you to see this bird. I told him that you are very busy and that you may not... [pause] ah yes of course, one moment Sir", the Colonel looked at me and said, "Bombardier where and what time do you want to meet the CRA?" I informed the CO of the time and place where I would meet him. After telling the CRA the details, the Colonel hung up and expressed his amazement that the Brigadier would want to go with me to "see a bloody owl". I walked away with a smile on my face. Again, the Colonel was right I did not get many people joining my 'club', I got just one person and that person was none other than the boss of my boss, how cool is that.

When I first met Wolf and Andreas, they told me that they could not speak English so over the years I was forced to learn German. This was made easier because of our common interest in birds. Some of the other soldiers in my unit played football with local teams, they learnt to speak German that way, like me because of their shared interest

German was easier to learn. Friday came, we picked up the CRA and off we went to the Arnsberger to trap and ring some Tengmalm's Owls. To stand a chance of ringing this owl we needed to get there for about midnight and stay until about three in the morning. It was so dark in the forest that you could not see your hand in front of your face. My job that evening was to translate for the CRA. I was doing really well, and I felt pleased with myself. Then after some time the CRA asked another question, and Wolf answered him in English. This is how that conversation went, in English:

Geoff:	"Wolf"
Wolf:	"yes Geoff"
Geoff:	"you just spoke English"
Wolf:	"yes I know"
Geoff:	"When I first met you, you told me that you could not speak English"
Wolf:	"yes, that's right"
Geoff:	"so, you've let me struggle with speaking German for the last three years, when you could have spoken to me in English"
Wolf:	"yes, it worked though, your German is good now"
Geoff:	**"I don't bloody care if it worked...".**

Wolf was right though, it did work. My face must have been a picture, if you could have seen it in the pitch black and the CRA found it highly amusing. Sometime after this trip I was called to the Battery Office (Admin), as I walked in to the office my BC Maj Pye informed me that the CRA was on the phone in his office; he wanted to speak with me. As I left to take the call, he said to me "I am not sure how I feel about one of my junior NCO's (non-commissioned officer) cavorting with the Brigadier". Without thinking, I replied don't worry sir, play your cards right and I will put in a good word for you.

The Army Ornithological Society (AOS), consists of serving and ex-serving members of the British Army. While in The Gambia with the AOS; we carried out a major river bird survey. Prior to sailing on a large riverboat, we had to attend a reception at the British High Commission in Banjul where we met various dignitaries. I was having a beer with Richard and some of the other members of the AOS when, an attractive woman walks straight up to me and said, "you are sleeping with me tonight". I immediately responded with, "I am happy with that, when do we leave". Wide-eyed she smiled and walked away. Richard with his face buried in his hands shaking his head, clarified "Geoff, it is her holiday village we are staying in tonight", "oh dear" said I, what a Muppet (Idiot).

We sailed from outside the capital all the way up to the border with Senegal. Along the way we saw birds like the Giant Kingfisher, White-backed Night Heron, African Fish Eagle, and African Finfoot, skulking along the edge of the river bank under some overhanging branches, what a great find. As for Black Kites, we stopped counting them in the end as there were so many of them. After several days on the river we pulled into a tourist campsite for a twenty-four-hour rest period. Soon after going ashore, my friends were eager to go straight out to find as many birds as possible. I declined to go; my sense was that the guys would not see anything of interest. The Expedition Leader and I had a good chat instead. She said afterwards that she was missing the spiritual connection with likeminded people whilst living in Africa.

The guys returned disappointed having not seen anything. Later that night, we were told where we could find a Verreaux's Eagle Owl, it was roosting in a nearby Giant Plum Tree. When I heard the word 'giant', I thought of a very large tree. That night, I dreamt of a vast wood on the horizon, I did not realise what relevance this was to have, not until later in the day. As I arrived for breakfast, all of the guys apart from Hilary Nash (an AOS member) were rushing out of the door to go and look for the Eagle Owl. After breakfast with Hilary we went to look for the owl as well. On route, we bumped into the others who had been unsuccessful in locating the owl and were now heading off to find Sand Grouse. They asked if we were coming but I said that I would meet up with them later. I felt that I just needed to connect with the trail, and enjoy what nature had to offer me. We then parted company. Shortly after this I saw a large wood in the distance, just like the one I had in my dream. As Hilary and I slowly headed towards the woodland, we paralleled a tree on our left, I had a sense that the owl was in this tree. As I approached it with caution, a large owl took flight from within the tree. I could not contain my excitement as I watched it fly towards the distant woodland. It was then that I realised that this tree was the Giant Plum Tree. When I thought the Plum Tree would be very large in size, it was in fact only about ten metres in height.

Perhaps this was why the other guys missed it, not realising the Giant Plum Tree was not such a Giant after all. Hilary and I soon located the Eagle Owl and we enjoyed magnificent views of it before setting off to let the others know where it was. On the way back to meet the guys, Hilary and I talked about how we could wind them up and keep them dangling for a while before telling them where it was. Our banter consisted of saying things like, "you know you wanted to pay someone to find the owl for you, well we found it! And it will cost you X amount!" that's when I realised that my banter began to sound like one-upmanship.

As Hilary and I continued talking it seemed with each word it became less important to get one over on the others, as I became more and more aware of my ego. We eventually met up with the others, and told them where they could find the owl with no strings attached, and off they set to bag it. A short while later one of the guys returned saying they could not locate it, and would we show them where it is. We eagerly showed everyone where the owl was located, it gave me great joy seeing the pleasure they had in seeing it.

It was great to share some quality time with Hilary too. Later I reflected on the words 'Eagle Owl' and what they might mean. Based on the Native American philosophy, that there is a spirit that moves through all things, the word Eagle represents Spirit, while the word Owl represents Deception; food for thought. Other notable birds that we saw on the trip were an Egyptian Plover; this bird is often referred to as the crocodile bird for its symbiotic relationship with crocodiles. We also bagged, Pearl-spotted owlet, a Marsh Owl flying overhead, an African Harrier-hawk, and a pair of Northern White-faced Scops Owls.

The guys were a bit miffed with me because I did not call them quick enough for the Scops Owls, although in my defence I thought they had seen them, sorry guys. Not a bird, but none the less it was a great find, on the border between Gambia and Senegal there was a roost of Yellow-winged bats. They are one of only five species of False Vampire bats and unlike other false vampires, the yellow-winged feeds only on insects. Before driving back to the capital, we decided to take a short boat trip into Senegal just so we could say that we had been there.

The Everglades was where I encountered my first Barred Owl. When I think of this bird it reminds me of an article that had been sent to me by an American friend; it was about a man who wanted to take photographs of Barred Owls. It seems that this enthusiastic bird photographer had decided that he would take photos of this owl during the nesting season. He set off with his camera, binoculars and a tape recorder, he eventually found a Barred Owl which was nesting close to a broad walk. He set his camera up and so that he could get a good photo, he wanted to draw the owl closer by playing a tape recording of the owl's call. However, as a direct result of playing the recording, the owl attacked him and drew blood. He then decided that he would sue the National Park for allowing a wild bird to nest too close to a public broad walk.

I was surprised by this; I had to do a double take on the date of the newsletter just to make sure it was not April fool's day. As I have said I have trapped and ringed owls in the wild many times; on one occasion I received a cut by a Tawny Owls razor sharp talon, because I closed my hand-held net too soon as she flew into it. In my opinion the photographer was in the wrong. If you go playing a tape recording of another owl in an established territory, especially when they have young, you are going to be attacked because they will see you as an intruding owl. The shocking part for me was that his complaint was upheld and as a direct result of his actions the park banned all electronic equipment from being used in the park. I am unsure if this ban still stands today. Barred Owls respond really well to what might be going on in the woods around them, and they are curious enough to fly in closer to see what is going on.

I was in Alberta, Canada at the largest military training base in the Commonwealth, known as the British Army Training Unit Suffield (BATUS); this is also Blackfoot country. The training area is 19% of the size of my home country, Northern Ireland and it is also a fantastic area for birds. BATUS is where we take part in an exercise called Medman (Medicine Man). This is an all-arms battlegroup exercise, which uses live ammunition. The units that took part in 1990/91 were being deployed to the Gulf. Located just on the outskirts of camp is a small lagoon for waste to run into; this proved to be an oasis for the wildlife. I saw plenty of birds there, from the Black Duck to the Palm Warbler. There was some run off from the lagoon which flowed down into a reedbed, and this was home to many species such as the Western Marsh Harrier, Short-eared Owl, and I once saw a Say's Phoebe on the rock face behind the reedbed. There were of course the usual birds like Red-winged Blackbirds, Yellow-throats and Common Nighthawks would fly over the lagoon at dusk, swooping down to catch a drink before going on to hunt for their food.

One day I was watching the Short-eared Owl quartering the reeds; after some time, I became aware of movement in my peripheral vision. I dropped my binoculars to get a better look at what was going on, and that's when I saw more movement in the distance, coming from different directions. I soon became aware that this movement belonged to a pack of Coyotes. They seemed to be making their way along the top of the rock face, then dropping down behind and around the reedbed. I turned to see where the owl had gone when I saw another Coyote, this one was sitting and watching me, it was some fifty metres away.

I looked around some more, only to realise that I was in fact being surrounded by them. I decided to turn sideways toward the closest Coyote and slowly walk away from this situation. I have no idea what their intent was, but I was not going to hang around to find out. I had the pleasure of doing several tours in Canada; in fact, it was a double pleasure as I have family in and around Calgary. Prior to going onto the prairie for our training, we were given a briefing by our Canadian hosts and part of the briefing was on conservation. We were shown some slides, one of which was of a Burrowing Owl and we were told that if we saw this bird, we had to report it straight away to the Eagle

Owl authorities who would then stop the exercise and move us to another part of the prairie. This was so that they could protect the owl. One night, I was returning to our Gun Position with my driver when I spotted six Burrowing Owls near to our location. I made a note of the grid reference and on arrival I went straight to the Command Post (CP) and informed the CP officer of my observation. I asked him to report the location to the Canadians. He responded by saying "you are joking aren't you" to which I replied, "do I look like I am joking Sir, please send the message". He replied, "I am not F%@king sending this". I asked him in front of the crew if he was refusing a direct request from our Canadian hosts. He glared at me, knowing that he had no choice now but to send it.

The Canadians were true to their word, they stopped the exercise and it took three days to relocate the Battle Group. Upwards of six hundred personnel, their vehicles and their equipment were relocated to another part of the range. I am sure the Officers were not best pleased with me, perhaps due to the loss of training time. On the upside though, I got some unexpected birding in, three days to be exact. This is what I would call a real moment of 'More Birds than Bullets' considering we were on a live firing exercise. During his dine out speech prior to leaving the army, BSM Graham Stacey expressed that in all his years in the army he have never known anyone to stop a battle group from moving, "Except for that F%@king TWITCHER, because of a F%@king BIRD" as he pointed in my direction. I felt quite honoured. I was also expecting to be spoken to by senior officers in my Regt, but it never transpired.

In my experience most British Soldiers are animal lovers, if not then they certainly have and do show compassion for wildlife wherever they encounter it; all except the ant killers. In one Gun Position Tiffy pulled up with his ARRV (Armoured Recovery and Repair Vehicle) within feet of a Hen Harriers nest. I walked over to him and asked if he would move his ARRV, because it threatened the nest. He looked at me as if I was off my head, until I showed him how close he was to the nest. Seeing the nest, he moved his vehicle without any hesitation. (Tiffy is an "artificer" which refers to a Senior Non-Commissioned Officer. Artificer is a job title and not a rank and they are usually called Tiffy). The ant killers I referred to, was a group of soldiers who were setting ants alight with lighter fuel; That was until I asked if I could have a go at it. Having handed me the fuel I sprayed one of them with the fuel and set him alight. They thought I was crazy, not as crazy as I thought they were.

A year after the Berlin wall came down in 1991; British Military personnel were allowed to go into the former Eastern Bloc. Richard and I took the opportunity to experience birding in the East, before it was lost to deforestation and development. Setting out from Germany we visited Austria, Hungary, Czechoslovakia (now the Czech Republic), Slovakia, Poland (via the Tatra Mountains) and into former East Germany.

We first arrived at Neusiedler See in Austria, bordering Hungary. The lake is Europe's second-largest steppe lake and it's found at the lowest point in Austria. We saw some cool birds while there like the Moustached and Barred Warblers.

During the first night in the hills near to Neusiedlersee, we heard a Eurasian Pygmy Owl and later on we dutifully reported our sighting to the guy in charge of the nature centre. As I relayed our sighting in my best German (or so I thought) he became very excited, he recorded our sighting in his logbook; informing us that our sighting was a first for that region. It was not until we were some way into Hungary, I said to Richard I got my German mixed up, we reported seeing a Scops

Owl; the German name for this bird is Zwergohreule and literally translated it means Dwarf Ear Owl. The owl we had heard is called Sperlingskauz in German; translated it means Sparrow Owl. I just hope that no 'Twitcher's' went to see our not so rare owl sighting.

We arrived at the Hortobágy National Park in eastern Hungary which covers an area of around 800 km2. It was designated a National Park in 1973 the first in Hungary. It is also Hungary's largest protected area of continuous natural grassland and the largest in Europe. We met a couple of local birders who had split a pair of binoculars into two halves and used them as individual scopes mounted onto wooden poles. I guess, this was perhaps due to the cost of a pair of Bins at that time and it would have been difficult for them to get hold of a modern pair. It just shows that when you want to do something you will find a way to achieve the best results with what you have available. As we chatted to them with our backs to a large reedbed, we asked them if they had seen any Black Storks.

They pointed behind us and said, "like that one you mean". We turned just as a magnificent Black Stork was gliding in to land amongst the reeds. Red-footed Falcons were everywhere, but sadly, we dipped on the Great Bustard; we encountered a British guy who had seen them just before we arrived. He asked us if we had heard their call before, we said "no". He then played his tape at which point we burst out laughing as it sounded like someone breaking wind. I suggest that you check out its mating call on the internet for yourself. We continued our journey and along the way we came across lots of discarded military equipment and empty soviet barracks. We even passed a scrap dealer where two MiG-21's (supersonic interceptor jet fighters) were laid on top of a load of old cars, still with their insignia on them.

During our drive through Hungary Richard and I were chatting when he came up with an idea, for the more extreme members of the AOS. He thought they should be called CAOS, instead of AOS; meaning the Continuity Army Ornithological Society as opposed to the Continuity Irish Republican Army (CIRA) who split from the Provisional Irish Republican Army (PIRA) in 1986. In other words, a few of the members from the AOS were considered a splinter group, the more extreme element of the AOS you might say. Especially when it came to the places they would travel to and the time spent birding; namely dawn until dusk.

By now it was getting dark, so we pulled into a car park, next to a residential estate in order to get our heads down for the night. I woke Richard up in the early hours of the morning to tell him about the blindly obvious White Storks, that were clapping their bills together from their nests; which were on top of the houses around us. Each house had installed wagon wheels on their roofs for the Storks to build their nests on. It is fair to say Richard was not very happy with me for waking him up, I guess he was tired from all the driving he had done, and I had not been very considerate towards him. After breakfast we continued with our drive through Eastern Europe, at one point we observed a clever way of using an old transport plane. The front half of the fuselage was cut away from the rest of the plane and then it was stuck onto the top floor of a restaurant. To get into the restaurant you had to walk up the steps, along the inside of the aircraft to get to your table; quite an novel idea.

At one point Richard and I considered the possibility of going into the Ukraine but as we got closer to the border, we felt it might be wiser to give it a miss. I guess on that occasion we were not so extreme after all, and so began a long night drive northward to the Tatra Mountains on the Czechoslovakian (now Slovakia) side.

We stopped at various points along the way in the hope of getting a Tengmalm's Owl by using a playback of its call. During one of the stops we had a response from another owl which we determined to be a Strix of unknown origin (Strix is a genus of owls in the family Strigidae), one of the two generally accepted living families of owls, the other being the Barn-Owl (Tytonidae). Prior to venturing into the wood to find this owl, we heard the roar of a Brown Bear in the distance, sadly we did not get any sightings of bears. We entered the woodland and soon realised that the wood was extremely boggy, forcing us to walk along fallen trees for fear of doing a disappearing act under all the mud and water.

As we approached the owl on top of a large fallen tree, our torch batteries started to run low, and just before they died, we saw IT, our first Ural Owl. We were overjoyed by our encounter with this awesome looking bird and we discovered on our return that the British Birds magazine had reported on the status of the birds in Czechoslovakia. Our Ural Owl was one out of ten known breeding pairs in the country. You could say we found the proverbial 'needle in the haystack'. On top of that we also bagged a European Three-toed Woodpecker the next morning as we walked along one of the mountain trails.

Coming down on the Polish side of the Tatra Mountains, we arrived at the border checkpoint where one of the border guards took away our passports and held them for over an hour. His colleague searched our car, and as he looked in the boot, he saw our military sleeping bags, bergen's and a few other military items. He looked at us inquiringly, pointing at our stuff. We said we were birdwatchers, to which he replied, "they all used to say that"; we figured that he meant spies.

He gave us the strong impression that he would not let us into the country until we had paid him. We informed him that all we had was local currency; we had been changing our money as we passed through each country. He was convinced that we had Deutschmarks or Dollars on us, and he was keen to get his hands on them. I had heard from friends that it was common practise for the border guards to ask for money, and here he was asking for it, perhaps in the belief that we were rich and could afford it.

However, when they saw us roll out our sleeping bags and started brewing up a pot of tea at the side of their hut. They let us in; perhaps realising that we were in it for the long haul. After our very unwelcome reception, we decided not to stay in Poland and pushed on into the former East Germany. We were aiming for the Gülper See, we saw six Ospreys, a Goshawk and one White-tailed Eagle. I love to watch Osprey's diving, I remember seeing my first one in Aviemore which is situated within the Cairngorms National Park in the Highlands of Scotland, what a beautiful place that is. While I was there a young Osprey turned up at my local patch, Abberton Reservoir for three days; if only I had known.

The osprey has several amazing adaptations that suit its piscivorous lifestyle as carnivorous animal that eats primarily fish. It folds its wings back seconds before entering the water to catch its prey; their outer toes are reversible, and they have sharp spicules a needle like structure on the underside of their toes for gripping their prey. They can also close their nostrils to keep water out when diving. They also have backwards facing scales on their talons which act as barbs allowing them to hold onto their catch and finally their dense oily plumage prevents their feathers from getting waterlogged, all in all a truly well adapted and amazing hunter. We also had to make a quick getaway over the Polish border into Germany. This was because some people tried to wash our windscreen, we told them not to wash it, but they did anyway. Richard drove off and because we had not paid them, they chased us down the road trying to kick the car. We had to laugh.

In Czechoslovakia we had bought some snacks and orangeade which turned out to be the most disgusting drink we have ever tasted. Some guy even tried to sell us an old-style blood pressure machine. I guess he needed to make a living in whatever way he could; with a deep sense of gratitude, that's when I realised how lucky I am. We gave the orangeade to our friend Dave Denton (an Ex RAF guy who runs his own business in Germany) as a gift for feeding us when we stopped over at his place on our way home. We were long gone by the time he had put his lips to the bottle. He called us to let us know that he was not very impressed with the drink, he used a few choice words as well; we so pissed ourselves laughing. We had also bought ice-cream from the same place as the orangeade, they were advertising ice-creams on the sort of board you would find at home; namely, 'Tom Selleck's' (Magnum's) and all sorts of other ice-creams. However, they only had one kind, and you really needed the orangeade to wash it down. It was like frozen powdered milk, that's the only way I can describe it. The best was yet to come when I arrived home, the house was empty. I thought where could my wife and kids be? Ah I know, they will be round Terry Farrows house, a friend of ours, Terry is one the nicest guys you could ever wish to meet, a gentle giant of a man. I knocked on their door; Pat, Terry's wife answered. She looked at me wide-eyed, open mouthed and in shock at seeing me standing there, she said "what are you doing here? We thought you had forgotten all about it". Think Geoff, think, what had I forgotten, my mind raced for answers, then my mouth let loose these words. "Why do you think I have come back early, it is because I have not forgotten", whatever it was, I had forgotten.

On entering their house, I was greeted with the same words from my wife and girls, "we thought you forgot" and my response was "who me? Never" I was able to string this out for well over an hour, that was until we were on the way home. Gabby, my wife at the time said to me, "you have forgotten, haven't you?" there was a silent pause. I confessed, "Yes, what have I forgotten?" she replied, "our wedding anniversary".

While out birding at the 'Zach' I was walking along with my head buried in my bird guide when I had to stop due to a low hanging branch. I looked up and literally inches in front of my face were two juvenile long-eared owls looking back at me, moving and turning their heads from side to side and upside down almost. I looked around but could not locate the adults, I did not stay long as I did not want to disturb them.

At around two in the morning I received a call from Gary (Brick) Copper a member of Dragon Battery. I thought we were getting called out, as it was around this time call outs would happen. Brick was on duty in the ammunition compound, having discovered an injured Barn Owl. He called to see if I would come and rescue it. I collected the owl and brought it home; I placed it in a box with a blanket to keep it warm and left it overnight to settle down. It appeared to have a broken wing so the likely hood of saving it was limited. The next morning it was still alive, I gave my wife a number to call and to ask them to come and collect it, I then went off to work. A few hours later she called to say it had died. When I got home, we took it to the Zach to bury it. On the drive back home, my wife and daughters were crying their eyes out; suddenly my wife said, "you are not to go back and dig it up, to get it stuffed" I thought Shit she's a F%@king mind reader, because that is exactly what I was thinking, I thought it would make a great display for school children. Needless to say, I did not go back.

While on a Med Man Exercise, Dave Horrobin found a dead Great-horned Owl on a track, he asked me if I wanted it. Of course, I said yes. I attempted to take it back to Germany to have it mounted. I put it in a plastic bag and placed it in a freezer in the main cookhouse on the QT, (the phrase means to be quiet about something, confidential or off the record). Sadly, when I came to collect it, it had gone. I found out later that the Master Chef had discovered it and went completely mental (understandably) and he threw it away.

My Elusive Bird

The Firecrest
I saw my first one just outside my office window in 2010.

CHAPTER 3

Bird Language

It was between two and three in the morning and we had been on the run for days. The full moon was casting shadows over the surrounding countryside, the air was fresh and crisp. I love being out at night as I feel like I am the only person around, but of course I am not, there were three other guys in our patrol. As we broke out from the shadows into the moonlight pasture, I looked across the field, over the hedgerows, and in the distance stood an old farmhouse. The light from one of its windows cut through the darkness, and even though it was cold, I felt warm inside.

I cast my eyes over the surrounding area looking for the enemy. Not far away the chimes from the local church broke the silence of the night. My senses were heightened; there was a live enemy with dogs trying to track us down.

We had to avoid capture, while they searched for signs of us; maybe a track or two, or locals letting them know that some food had gone missing from their land. They would be seeking to cut us off at the pass, so to speak, as they checked railway stations for signs of us trying to gain ground quickly.

Observation posts were deployed to watch over large open areas, to see if anyone was daft enough to break cover and cross the open ground; we were four nights into the escape and evasion phase of our Battlefield Survival course. The course was run by 22 SAS at the International Long-Range Reconnaissance Patrol School (ILRRP) in Weingarten, Germany.

I was alerted by an alarm call from a Blackbird. It was coming from behind us. Realising that something or someone was close by, I raised my concerns with the rest of my patrol that someone might be following us, but they completely dismissed the idea. As we continued our journey, I was still aware of the continuing alarm calls. I was convinced that we were being tracked by Special Forces, as this was a Special Forces school, it made sense to have another course track us to improve on their tracking skills. I didn't get confirmation as to whether we were being followed, however I completely trusted what the birds were telling me. On many levels my awareness had been pricked, first the blackbirds and then the rest of the animal world that were responding to the concentric rings were sending out as we moved across the land.

Interpreting bird language is in itself an art form; their calls, postures and behaviour convey information. According to Jon Young, author of 'What the Robin Knows'. 'The attentive, trained observer can deduce through bird language the location of predators and other forces on the landscape'; this is also my experience and that of my friends who practise bird language. Since reading Jon's book my eyes have been opened to other possibilities and shed light on my past experiences, allowing me to understand the process of what was happening back then by joining the dots together. The alarm call of the Blackbird to the untrained ear is just that, an alarm call. To an experienced ear, the Blackbird alarm changes slightly to warn us of different threats. Be it an approaching dog or cat, someone walking a dog and of course a human (or humans), the blackbird has a slightly different alarm for each of the above. I have experienced it with Magpies in response to a fox. My friend G and I were walking along the edge of a wood, talking about the tracking course we were running, when G spotted a fox moving across the field in front of us. As it headed into the wood to our left, the Magpies kicked off. We noticed that the call of the Magpies for the fox was different to the alarm they would give for a human. It was quite distinct as I recall, we were able to track the fox purely by listening to where the Magpies were, and later they were joined by two Jays. It would be true to say that back then (in the army) I could not distinguish the subtle variations within an alarm, nonetheless I was aware of danger because the birds were alerting me to it. You may recall a documentary about gophers on the prairie and how their alarms differ according to each of the differing threats, basically it's similar in birds.

ILRRP was one of the most powerful courses I have ever done; as a patrol we did not get on well with each other. I believe that had we got on well, we would have learnt a lot, but nowhere near as much as I learnt about myself and others because of the simple fact that we did not get along.

When I first heard the term 'Bird Language' I thought that it was a reference to a bird's song and in part I was correct. I remember on one occasion, Feathers (Alex), Green Pete (Peter) and I were hiding in the undergrowth on the edge of a wood prior to stalking in on Thomas Schorr-kon's nature connection course. While we chatted amongst ourselves, I heard a Blue Tit alarming nearby, and having caught my attention, I asked the others to be quiet. I indicated that we were not alone, so we set out with stealth to find out what the cause of the alarm might be. Judging by the type of alarm, it was a human. It was not unusual for other friends to test their stalking skills on the hunter group (us). Lying low, we crawled out from our hiding place and came face to face with Phil, another scout who had indeed been stalking us. Phil Greenwood a former Royal Marine is an out-standing nature-connection teacher/mentor, and unfortunately for him, the Blue Tit alerted us to his presence, and he was sent packing to practise his stalking skills for another day – result!

At the end of a bird language course I attended in California, I managed to get some birding in. In order to get from where the course was held to San Francisco I had to pass over the iconic Golden Gate Bridge. This is where Star Fleet Command will be in the future. Yes, I am a fan of Star Trek. I spent the day birding along the coast. At one point I was walking alongside a reedbed, when a pair of Red-winged Blackbirds took position high up on some reeds, one either side of me and in close proximity, they were alarming. Suddenly, I clocked a Peregrine Falcon heading straight for me at speed. I could feel the down draft from its wings as it passed inches over my head.

Sometimes, birds will use humans for protection; from predators and on the flipside, predators can also use humans for hiding their approach from their prey, in the hope of improving their chances of making a kill. It was clear that these two Redwings were using me to protect themselves from an incoming Peregrine, while alerting other wildlife of the danger.

When I was driver training in Germany, I would often take my students all over the countryside, and away from towns; my reason for this was twofold. Firstly, the countryside is where the men would be doing a lot of their driving while on exercise and secondly, I could search areas looking for potential Barn Swallow roosts. Having found such a roost, I called Wolf and Karl to tell them about where I had found it; we arranged to go there and ring the Swallows.

We set up our nets around a maizefield. Once it was all setup, we switched on a tape recording of swallows calling, in order to lure them into the nets; then we stood back in a line along the road that ran parallel with the field and waited for them to land and roost for the night. The swallows gathered like a swarm of bees, swirling around us; having grabbed their last meal of insects, they began to settle down on the maize. Then unexpectedly they all took flight and formed a tight mass of swirling birds. We looked around realising that there must be a Hobby nearby looking for its last meal of the day. What happened next took us all by surprise. As we searched the sky trying to find the Hobby, I was astounded to see it fly between my legs! It then raced up towards the flock, reaching out, it grabbed a swallow and flew off. That was its evening meal taken care of! The important thing here, is that both predator and prey from time to time use humans for their own survival. I remember once Richard and I came across a Hobby catching Butterflies while several of its young watched on from a nearby tree. We guessed it was teaching them to hunt butterflies before upgrading to catching and eating Dragonflies on the wing, the precision and skill the adult bird displayed was awesome.

I was walking with a San Bushman in Namibia, when a European Roller flew overhead. The bushman with his arms outstretched whistled to the Roller, at the same time he moved his body in a way that appeared to be mimicking the roll of a Roller in flight. Then, right on cue the Roller, rolled. It seemed to me that they were both connected, and they were enjoying each other's company through the dance; the bushman clearly understood the language of birds.

We are all capable of this kind of connection and understanding, but with the distractions of our modern lives most of us have switched off to it. The connection the San have with their environment is something to behold; when they track an animal for example, they seem to become that animal. There is a clip of the San tracking a Kudu in David Attenborough's 'Life of Mammals' documentary. It shows the San tracking on so many different levels, not just physical tracking but energy tracking as well; this is because of their understanding of the birds and animals that they live with.

I lived in a cave for about four days on the coastline on the Isle of Islay. I even found a coconut, which lived at the entrance to my cave. Jeremy Hastings of Islay Bushcraft and I shared stories and experiences, we also exchanged ideas on Nature Connection and Tracking. One day we waded into the ocean, to collect some wild food such as mussels and other shellfish which we found clinging to rocks. We cooked the handful that we had collected, and I have to tell you, after having only eaten one small mussel, my body felt energised throughout. I felt like I did not need to eat anymore. Straight from the sea, you could not get fresher than that, this was a first for me.

On our return home it soon became clear how relaxed we had become due to living out in the wilds. As we birded on our way back, I said to Jeremy, "I feel a Golden Eagle coming on" and Jeremy agreed that it would round the week off nicely. We were not disappointed; Jeremy spotted a Golden Eagle soaring in the distance. Adopting the prone position, we watched this magnificent bird for some considerable time. Then, I heard a Whimbrel calling, it was to the front of us and moving around to our right. Jeremy was about twenty feet in front of me. I decided to imitate its call, by whistling loudly, and immediately I got a response back. I whistled again, and once again it responded. The whole time it continued to move around to the right of us. I gave another whistle and sure enough the Whimbrel responded again. I was aware that it had passed behind us, but now it had changed direction and was heading back towards us. The calling continued while Jeremy and I continued to stay in the prone position.

The Whimbrel was getting closer and closer. The whole time my eyes were firmly fixed to my binoculars so that I did not miss out on the rare opportunity of seeing a Golden Eagle. I decided to look up from my bins, just in time to see the Whimbrel gliding in, 3-4 inches directly over Jeremy's head and landing just out of arms reach to the right of me. In all my years of birdwatching never have I been so close to a Whimbrel, not even the bright red and yellow plastic bags that contained our gonk bags (sleeping bags) on our backpacks bothered it.

I motioned to Jeremy to get the camera out, to which he rightly replied that this was not a camera moment. I would have loved a picture with the Whimbrel, but that is my EGO talking. In Alcoholics Anonymous (AA), EGO means Easing God Out. We spent some twenty minutes or more, watching the Whimbrel walk in and around us; there were just two very brief moments when the bird became alarmed. The first time, it lifted off the ground about twelve inches, it gave a single call and then landed immediately. The second time, it lifted a bit higher than before and gave two calls before landing again. I believe that this was because we had changed our mindset. At first, we were in what is known as baseline, this is when everything in nature is settled and normal, perhaps we were thinking that it was time to get going again, in other words we switched from a heart space into our heads.

Eventually we had to move on, at which point the Whimbrel took flight; it was hard to end what was undoubtedly a truly magical moment. Some months later I was running a course, and during the introductions one of my clients said she had a question for me. I invited her to ask it. Her question was "Golden Eagle or Whimbrel" I immediately beamed a big smile and replied, "without doubt, the Whimbrel". She had been on a course with Jeremy and he had told her this story and suggested she ask me that question.

The reason for being on Islay was to recce the location; with the view to bringing people with an addiction for some Wilderness Therapy. After the recce I returned a few months later with two counsellors from the rehab I worked for. The aim was to spend one night in the wilderness in order for them to experience what our clients would experience. As soon as we arrived on site, we showed them their cave; Jeremy and I slept across the way from them in another cave.

The next morning, I watched the counsellors chatting with each other; their body language was interesting to observe, I drew Jeremy's attention to it; we were not quite sure what to make of it. They then disappeared out of sight and we set about preparing breakfast. As I was frying some eggs I looked up and saw them heading back towards us; their body language this time looked like something out of the film 'Gunfight at the O.K. Corral'. I said to Jeremy check them out, they arrived by the campfire, and looking down at us one of them said "we have just seen your cave", I replied "is there a problem?" to which the response was, "your cave is bigger than our cave". My god, I said, "guys you have only been out twenty-four hours and already you have gone Neanderthal on us".

Sitting in nature by a tree or indeed in the open by the sea is a good way to just be. I have had many Sit-spots in various locations and habitats around the world. Perhaps one of the most profound was in Bosnia in 1996 where I served as part of the first NATO troops to be deployed there. My Sit-spot was a small bushy area on the bend of a fast-flowing river. This was on the boundary of a factory complex in which we were based. I used this Sit-spot to escape the confines of the camp and sometimes I just needed some down time away from the environment we found ourselves in. At times I could hear people calling for me; sometimes I would ignore them. Lighting up another cigarette, I would carry on with my sit-spot; I knew that whatever the problem was they would have sorted it by the time I got back to the office. I shared this with my boss Ken Barma. Ken took to joining me when he could; we would chat about life and birds. I enjoyed that quality time with him.

As I relaxed in my sit-spot, I watched a Dipper fly past, a Grey Wagtail was on the far bank searching for food among the rocks at the water's edge, bobbing its tail up and down. Nearby, I could hear a Honey Buzzard calling, I knew there was a breeding pair around, as I had seen them almost on a daily basis. At the end of my sit-spot I went for a fag in the smoking area. I could still hear the Honey Buzzard calling; then my attention was drawn away from the sky and toward a bush near to where I was standing. I was expecting to see the Honey Buzzard, but instead I saw an Eurasian Jay, perfectly mimicking the Honey Buzzards call; I was impressed. I am always keen to explore new encounters and knowing that the Jay had fooled me, I realised that I need to continue to be aware of my surroundings on many levels. Some of the questions that came to mind after this encounter were: Was the Jay attempting to scare nesting birds into revealing their nest sites? Why had the Jay chosen to be in that particular place? Was it using the presence of humans in some way and if so, why? At the time I remembered that a few years before I followed a Golden Oriole which was calling from high up in the canopy. Its yellow colour would make it difficult to see against the sunlight. That was until I realised that a Jay was in fact the culprit, and I had no idea if it was having fun with me or not, I suspect it might have been. While out Langlaufing (cross-country skiing) one day with Ken, Nick Hook and our Battery Captain, I spotted the back end of an Eurasian Brown Bear as it made its way up hill, heading away from us.

As I said before the trip to Morocco was awesome, we were on the edge of the Sahara, the world's largest and one of the harshest deserts on the planet. At 3.6 million square miles (9.4 million square kilometres), the Sahara, which is Arabic for "The Great Desert," engulfs most of North Africa.

While looking for the Desert Warbler with our guide, I took advantage of one aspect of bird language. I decided to drop back from the main group, I knew that if they flushed the bird, it would hook back behind them. There was a fifty, fifty chance of it working; the strategy paid off. The warbler flushed, it hooked around to their left. I stood still to watch where it would go, it crossed the track in front of me and landed in some tall grass to my right. The main group had not seen it; once I confirmed it, as a Desert Warbler I called the others and they got to bag it as well. It was a beautiful bird, the smallest in its genus, measuring 11–12 cm long. It had a pale sandy yellow-brown upper body, similar in colour to the grass it had landed in; the bill and legs were yellowish, and its iris was a stunning yellow.

While sitting in my car making a phone call, I clocked a Sparrowhawk in my peripheral vision as it appeared from a driveway on my right. This male was flying inches from the ground, rising over the bonnet of my car, then dropping down to just a few feet above the road. It was oblivious to the fact it could have been hit by a car as it crossed the road. It raced off down another driveway still inches above the ground. After ten metres, it swooped up and over a wall with an inch or so to spare, dropping behind the wall and out of sight. I wonder if it caught what it was after.

We took a walk through the woods and ended up standing in the middle of a track. My client was sharing some very personal experiences when we were surprised by a Sparrowhawk flying between us. What was amazing about this experience was that it had brushed up against both of our legs as it passed between us. It continued accelerating as it flew down the track at just above knee height, unhindered by touching us. It banked to the right and up, without slowing down it weaved its way through the maze of branches that made up the dense tree canopy and disappeared.

On another occasion I was with a client when everything went quiet, apart from a blackbird alerting me to the presence of a dog and its owner. As we watched and listened, five Roe Deer appeared and stopped close to us, having checked us out they slowly moved away as if nothing had happened. A short while later a Jack Russell appeared followed by its owner. Another time in the same area I had a client doing a sit-spot. I went off to throw a concentric ring so that he could experience bird language in action, by watching how the birds responded to my presence in the woods. I went some distance down a track before moving into the woods well out of sight from him, so that he would have no idea where I was.

Moving slowly forward I spooked a female Red Deer; I had not seen her as she was in some dead ground just ahead of me. She ran off and disappeared over a rise, heading towards my client. I continued to throw a concentric ring when I spotted the same deer coming back towards me but moving off to the left. A while later I was getting very close to my client when he turned and saw me. Sitting down next to him. I asked what he had seen the birds doing in response to my presence. Instead of talking about the birds he told me of the Red Deer coming over the rise and stopping directly in front of him. He was in peripheral vision, and in the heart. The deer was looking at him, it then walked over to him and touched his nose with her snout. After a brief moment, showing no fear she walked away from him. I believe he will never forget that moment.

A sit-spot is a good way of increasing your skill base in relation to Bird Language, in order to understand what the birds are telling us. At the end of Jon Young's bird language course in the States, I could tell what all the birds were up too in the surrounding area, just by watching their comings and goings every day for a week. During one of our sit-spots I heard a clicking sound on a branch behind me, as I turned slowly to my right, I saw a Great-horned Owl leaving the wood behind me and making its way over to the next wood. The clicking sound must have been its talons hitting the branch as it landed. We discovered that as the owl returned to its roost the Coopers Hawk came out to hunt at the same time; it was like they were swapping shifts. Every day it was the same routine. On the last day we were gathered around the campfire giving our feedback on the course. Often on these courses people would break into song and this day was no exception.

There was drumming and guitars, and in between people shared their experiences of the course. During this time, we became aware of a bird that had been elusive to most of us all week, it was up and circling above our heads on a wonderful sunny day. It was as if he had come to say goodbye to us all and to join in the musical celebrations. The bird was the magnificent Cooper's Hawk.

While attending a course at the Tracker School in the Pine Barrens in New Jersey, in the USA; I was in my Sit-spot, when I became aware of a Red Squirrel up on a branch eating a nut a few feet away. It appeared completely unaware of my presence, or perhaps it was aware of me but did not view me as a threat. I had my energy pulled in and my awareness pushed out. A short while later a Browncreeper (which is in the same genus as our Treecreeper) broke cover from a wood opposite and crossed a clearing, which was eighty or so meters wide. It flew straight towards me at head height and landed on the tree I was resting against; having passed directly over my head. It was so close that I felt the gentle downdraft from its wings; I have never experienced such an event with what at times can be an elusive bird. The Red Squirrel suddenly jumped and gave out an alarm as it ran off across the branches triggering a series of alarm calls from other birds as it went. The squirrel had become aware of my presence when I switched from being in a relaxed heart-centred place and back into my head; caused by my excitement of having the Browncreeper land so close to my head. I had changed the base rhythm on an energetic level and was now sending out a concentric ring.

My driver Geordie Mayne (RIP) and I were driving to our gun position somewhere on the prairie, during a Med Man exercise. I looked out of my window and there was a Prairie Falcon flying parallel to our truck just below eye level. This stunning bird of prey stayed with us for at least half a mile, what a thrill. I suspected it was using our truck to mask its movements, in order to position itself for a run up to making a kill. Now, in location, I climbed out of my vehicle; I stood for a moment to have a good old stretch after the drive. As per normal I am always looking out for birds, it's in my DNA. What happened next, I really was not expecting, to my surprise a juvenile Golden Eagle appeared just over the raise which was twenty metres to my front. It passed within a few feet over my head, I turned and watched it glide off into the distance.

Holland is a cool place to bird, we did many trips there. Once Richard was playing the call of a Rosefinch. When we got no response, he put his CD player away, in that moment two Dutch birders came around the corner. They asked if we had heard the Rosefinch. Not having the heart to say that it was a playback we said yes, but we did not see it. Later we were watching waders and geese in a field; when from left to right they took flight, rising and landing quickly, it was like watching a wave in action. We did not see the cause of the alarm, but a good guess for it would be a Peregrine Falcon.

I took Merlin, my Eurasian Eagle Owl out for a stroll one day along the famous Tarka Trail which runs parallel to an estuary near to where I lived. During this time some twenty people, from cyclists to families out walking, stopped to ask questions about Merlin. They were completely captivated by him, I answered their questions, while Merlin looked around to see what food he could find. They were taking pictures, they stroked him, during this time they all had big smiles on their faces. Just by being in the presence of this powerful bird, the energy of the people had changed. As they walked away, I observed their interaction with each other and I overheard one boy saying, "I can't wait to show my friends the photos." I thought about the concentric rings that would be sent out to their family and friends when they told them of their encounter with Merlin. The next day I was talking to someone who I had only just met, he told me about a story he heard on the radio the day before. Someone had phoned in and told the DJ about their experience of meeting a bloke with an Eagle Owl along the Tarka Trail. He did not know that the story was about Merlin. Who knows how far that concentric ring went and how many other people Merlin brought joy to that day?

CHAPTER 4

More Birds Than Bullets

The stars shone magnificently in the clear night sky, it was coming up to midnight at Eringerfeld, and all around me Nightingales were singing; at first, I heard one or two but as time passed, more of them joined in. Singing their hearts out, the crescendo of their song was something to behold as the melodies drifted throughout the countryside. I have never heard so many Nightingales in one place, it was like being in your own personal concert. The orchestra was interrupted by the harsh rasping sounds, delivered by Corncrakes.

I have only ever glimpsed a single Corncrake, it popped its head into the road from a grass verge as I drove past, to hear so many was just awesome. They were in a field a short distance from me. It felt like heaven listening to these two cracking birds, their songs freed my mind of any intruding thoughts. I was enjoying being immersed in the moment.

In the distance, the faint rumbling sound of the guns shattered the peace as they approached my position. It was time to get to work; I jumped down from the top of my vehicle where I had been laying. I fired up the engines on my POD which is also known as a UBRE (Unit Bulk Refuelling Vehicle). The hoses were laid out, and cyalumes (military grade chemical light sticks) were deployed to help guide in the 27.5 tons of rolling steel, well, it was aluminium armour really. I was running a single fuel rolling replen (replenishment). A rolling replen is where the POD is static, and the vehicles drive past the POD to fill up as opposed to the POD driving around to fill up static vehicles. Different colour cyalumes are used in a multi-rolling replen, namely, Red = POL (petrol, oil and lubricants), Amber = Ammunition, Green = Rations plus Mail and Blue = Water).

Once the guns had refuelled, they moved off to their next gun position. As their sound drifted into the distance, I turned my attention back to the Nightingales and Corncrakes. I decided to resume my position back on top of the POD; I was in no rush to get back to camp. I lay there for a few more hours soaking up the sound, watching the shooting stars criss-crossing the moon lit, star filled night sky, and once again I was in Nirvana.

It came time to return to camp and as I drove down the road, I flushed lots of Tree Pipits from the road. Many small birds tend to use the roads to keep warm at night.

I was ringing Spotted Flycatchers with my friends at the Kurpark (Health Spa), in Bad Westernkotten near to the town of Lippstadt in Germany. Andreas and Wolf left me to get on with the birds we had in the bags, while they went to check on some of the other nest boxes that had been placed around the park for the flycatchers to nest in.

It was while I was colour ringing one of the flycatchers, an elderly lady came up to me waving her umbrella above her head, she looked quite angry, so much so, I thought she was going to strike me with her umbrella. She was shouting at me; telling me to stop being cruel to the birds. With my limited German, I introduced myself, surprised, she looked at me and said "you're not German". I replied, "no I am British, I am stationed here in Lippstadt". I went on to explain to her what we were doing and why we were doing it. Her whole demeanour changed, she smiled at me and said, "I think it is really wonderful that foreign people come to our country and take care of our German birds". I had to smile as did Andreas and Wolf when I told them what had happened.

Birds in the hand I have had a few. Mostly through trapping and ringing, however, others resulted from wild birds choosing to land on my hand, from a Florida Scrub Jay to a Mountain Chickadee. I suspect the first was as a result of human interaction because the Jay appeared to be looking for food and as I was in a tourist area this may well have been the case.

However, in the countryside of Boulder in Colorado with very few people around, I stretched out my arm and opened my hand flat; to my joy a Mountain Chickadee landed on my hand, even though I had no food to offer it. During this time, I also bagged three Red-headed Woodpeckers flying a short distance away. I spoke with a local birder about them and she said that they had not been seen around Boulder for over twenty years.

I visited my good friend Badger; who manages a wood in Devon. Arriving early, I parked up by the gate and started to walk up to where he was working. On the way I passed a Wren which was alarming, I thought nothing of it, believing that I was the cause of the alarm. I moved on. I was some way past it, yet it was still alarming. I became curious as to what might be setting it off, maybe it was a Stoat. It was creating such a fuss I returned to check out what was causing it to behave in this way.

I watched and listened, trying to find the source of the fuss, when a round black ear appeared from beneath the ferns directly in front of me. Suddenly it ran off; I did not see what it was. The wren then settled down and I carried on. Later, I went for a walk around the woods, then came the call of nature and as I moved into the undergrowth away from the track, I had a real sense of being watched and I had an image in my mind of a large black cat looking at me. At this point a Blackbird took flight from high up in a tree, it flew straight up and across the track, it looked like it was trying to get away from something.

I noticed that its alarm was different. Things settled down and I thought no more of it, that was, until that evening when Badger shared an experience he had had in the woods. He told me that he had seen a large black cat dragging a deer into the woods from a nearby field. At which point I had a light-bulb moment, realising the ear that I saw must have belonged to the same cat, the height of the ear from the ground suggested it was a large animal.

The only other time I had seen an unusual cat was while visiting another friend. It was dark and I was driving along a typical Devon country lane, a narrow road with high hedges either side of my car. At one point I stopped to check my map and when I looked up from the map, sitting in the road, what for all intents and purposes appeared to be a domestic cat. Except, its legs were much longer than a domestic cat and its tail was at least one and half times the length of its body. It had beautiful chocolate, velvet like brown fur with creamy flashes behind its ears, just like a tiger. I watched it clear the hedge with a single leap, I would have estimated the hedge to be around six to seven feet in height; I have no idea what kind of cat it was.

I was at the base of a rocky outcrop, walking along a track, which dropped some six feet as I past a line of trees on my left. At the end of the tree line I spotted a very exposed nest in one of the trees. As I watched the nest, a Yemen Linnet arrived to feed its young, until then the young were completely on their own.

After watching the adult feed its chicks, I headed back to the truck. I had only gone a few paces, when suddenly there was a commotion. I turned in response to the adults scolding cries; I saw a crow perched on the nest eating one of the young, in a short space of time all the chicks were gone.

Several questions sprang to my mind. Was the Crow already aware of the chicks in the nest? Did my presence expose the nest, which the crow then took advantage of? I have no real way of knowing, but what I do know now is that whenever I discover a nest I do not hang around, I move on quickly. There may be another possibility, I got chatting with one of the instructors on my bird language course in California.

He informed me that California Scrub Jays adopt and protect American Robin nests from other marauders. The reason appears to be that the Jays are kind of 'farming' the chicks, as they watch over the nest, they are waiting until the chicks are big enough, they then move in and eat the young. My other question is: do other corvids do the same?

Sennelager Military Training Area is under the control of the British Forces based in Paderborn Garrison, which is on the western edge of the Teutoburg Forest and covers an area of 116 square kilometres (45 sq. mi). While Scimitar's (an armoured reconnaissance vehicle) fired their rounds down the range, a Black Stork was chilling on its nest right next to the firing point. The Storks were not even disturbed by the rapid firing coming from the Scimitar's.

My CO informed me that the job of Conservation Officer for the range had become available and he felt I was the best person for the job. He asked me if I would be interested. I said "yes", I am very interested; I left his office feeling excited by the prospect. I saw it as a job for life, doing what I enjoy. The job eventually went to an officer who was about to retire. When the CO told me this, he was clearly unhappy, as was I.

One of my BC's was an entomologist and he was instrumental in collecting insects from the Falklands for the Natural History Museum; I believe one or two were named after him as well.

During a night deployment the gun position was on silent routine and strict control was placed on the use of lights. During these quiet hours the BC placed moth traps in the middle of the gun position, the light from the traps gave away our position. The guys often teased me for being a birdwatcher, they also teased the BC; I say teased, really, they just simply took the piss.

Sometimes he would climb into the command post and in front of him, lined up on his map table, were dead insects; other times, someone would come in and present him with a dead insect and ask him what species it was. Thankfully, he had a good temperament. I am just glad they did not do this with me, I am not so sure I would have been as forgiving if someone had presented me with a bird that they had killed, just to ask me what species it was. I might have responded with, "What I am looking at is a Homo Europenis, (translated you're a Dick) and of course I am referring to the man not the bird".

Karl and I were ringing Barn Swallows on a farm when the farmer came over and told Karl not to come back. When Karl asked why, the farmer replied, "you are just not welcome anymore", maybe it was because of Karl's Green Political views.

The following year Karl had a return on one of his leg rings, and amazingly it was from Mongolia. We were both taken aback by the fact that one of our swallows had made it so far. There was the view that Barn Swallows might cross over between the west and eastern ranges, but it was never proven, and this one return should not be considered proof either. We were also blown away by the fact that someone had found the ringed bird and handed the ring number in. It made the local newspaper and Karl did something crafty; he told the papers that the bird was ringed in the farm next to where it was actually ringed, and that farm belonged to the farmer that had banned Karl from his land. Sometime later, Karl received a phone call from this farmer inviting him back onto his land. It seems that when he went to the pub, all of his friends were telling him that he was famous because one of 'HIS' swallows had turned up in Mongolia. It was just a little white lie, but it did the trick and ringing on his farm recommenced. I knew someone from the Gambia; who told me that as a kid when he went sea fishing, often, he caught Terns on his fishing line and some of them would have leg rings. He would take the rings home and give them to his mother. She would then wear them as ear rings or as a neckless. I asked him the next time he went home would he record the ring numbers and give them to me.

While out trapping swallows in Nordrhein-Westfalen (NRW), we were close to the Hamm Reactor. I went for a stroll along the riverbank where I discovered a family of Egyptian Geese, which turned out to be the first breeding record for NRW.

Another time we were out trapping and ringing Sand Martins. Having just ringed a Sand Martin, we released it only to watch it fly centimetres above the water as it headed back to its roost on the far side of the Baggersee (Gravel pit). We all stood at the water's edge willing it on, I was worried as a result of our actions we had put the bird under stress, which caused it to struggle as it returned home.

Thankfully three quarters of the way over the water it started to gain height, eventually it made it across, to a huge sigh of relief from all of us. We returned some weeks later only to discover that a Beech Martin/s had raided all the nests; except for two.

After the 1st Gulf war, Richard and I had arranged to go birding for the day in Holland with our friend Dave Denton. After climbing into our car, the first words out of Dave's mouth were "well, what was the war like?", Richard and I just looked at each other. Richard replied, "Dave you saw much more on television than we did; anyway, there was this Squacco Heron in the middle of the desert". I added that I dipped out on an Eagle Owl at the ammo compound, but I made up for the lack of birding that day by sunbathing on top of the truck where I had found my men, also sunbathing. They had decided to take some time out and not rush back to Kuwait; I don't blame them. David could not believe what we were saying, so much so he told his work colleagues about his experience with us.

As part of settling back into our normal routine that is military life, Richard and I decided that we would have some R&R (rest and recuperation) with our friend Mick. The Camargue was where we headed.

The Camargue is a birders paradise, and on arrival we were given a magnificent flying display by a flock of European Bee-eaters; with the sunlight reflecting off them they were like a rainbow with wings. Soon after the Bee-eaters display, we picked up some Stone Curlews and from there the day just got better and better.

Before heading up to Mont Ventoux, which was two hours northeast of the Camargue, on route we parked up and camped out for the night. Mick had brought with him an Iraqi NVG's (night vision goggles) that he had brought back from the Gulf. Our night was eventful because directly above our heads was a group of Beech Martens; we managed to get fleeting glimpses of these magnificent animals through the NVG's as they moved over the branches above us.

After breakfast, we did a little bit more birding before continuing onto Mont Ventoux to look for the Citril Finch. On arrival Richard realised that he had left his bins on the car roof; thankfully Mick had a spare pair in his glovebox. According to Richard the bins were not very good, but still, we all got to see the finch and a cracking little bird it was too. When I first met Mick, Richard had put him in touch with me. Mick was keen to see a Montagu's Harrier, after meeting up at my place we headed for Eringerfeld. We pulled up near to a barn where a Barn Owl lived. In the time that we were there we counted over 60 harriers, namely Marsh, Montagu's and Hen Harriers. The Marsh Harriers were the most abundant and the Montagu's was a breeding bird. We were there at the right time of year as the Hen Harriers were moving in and the Montagu's were moving out to head south for the winter. I also took him to see our resident European Eagle Owl in a nearby quarry.

In 1999 I took part in a trek in the Sinai desert to help raise funds for Mencap. We walked for five days guided by Bedouin and Israeli guides. Sleeping under the stars each night in the desert is a wonderful and very powerful place to be. Many people think that there is nothing there and yet when you take the time to sit and just be in the moment, you will see that the desert is full of life. We encountered snakes, birds and lizards, and people riding their camels going we knew not where, but they appeared very relaxed in their travels.

Along the way we stopped to pay our respects to our servicemen and women who fought and died for us in the wars. The Bedouin were very respectful during this period, except for one young man who was immediately chastised by the chieftain. We each laid a stone on a rock as a symbol of our respect, it was Remembrance Day. Afterwards everyone went about their business. I on the other hand, I had to walk away out of sight as I had become emotional, after I had recovered myself I returned to the group who were none the wiser of what had taken place; the only person who was aware of my emotional state was the chieftain from the Bedouin. As the group lined up for their lunch, I saw the chieftain looking at me through the legs of the group, sitting with my back to a rockface, we made eye contact; he bowed his head ever so slightly in my direction. I returned the bow, knowing he understood, that was a moment of spiritual connection and a special moment of human connection.

During the walk there was not much opportunity to bird; that said while we rested under an acacia tree I heard a bird calling, looking up I saw it was a Blackstart, it gets its name from the colour of its tail, which it frequently fans out, and flicks from side to side, it was a lovely little bird and one I did not expect to find.

We reached Mount Sinai; everyone except me wanted to visit the monastery. Jane, who I had made friends with wanted to go to the monastery, to do this she needed to cover up. She asked if I would look after her cut-off jeans for her, I took them and put them in my backpack. I had decided that I would walk up the mountain, not by the camel route but by the direct route, which was straight up. I was hoping for and got a Tristram's Grackle and Sinai Rosefinch, two lovely birds.

After spending some time on the mountain, we made our way back down and boarded our transport for Israel. On our way into Israel we stopped for something to eat and while I was enjoying my chips, a bird tried to steal some from my plate. It was none other than a Tristram's Grackle and that's what I call Sod's Law; you hike up a mountain to see what you think is a hard bird to find and then it only goes and turns up on your dinner table. That's why I always say, "never say never with birds, they have a habit of proving you wrong".

We climbed aboard our bus again and headed into Eilat. At the border crossing Jane asked for her jeans back, I suggested that she wait until we got to the hotel, but she asked again. I said "no, wait until we get there"; she became insistent. I said "Jane, you can't have them, you see that smoked glass over there? Well, they will be watching us and if I give you your jeans, they will think there is something odd going on". Just then, I was called forward.

I was the first in the line to be questioned by the border guards. Now it is fair to say that when it comes to authority, I can be a bit of a pain in the backside. Every time the guard asked me a question, I would interrupt her, for example:

Border Guard: "did you pac…"
Me: "YES"
Border Guard: "did anyone give yo…"
Me: "NO"
Border Guard: "what's in this Bott…"
Me: "WATER"

Eventually, she let me go and once everyone cleared customs, we got on the bus and headed for our hotel. I was in my room unpacking when Jane walked in, my roommate upped and left quickly. I know now that he knew the whole story, hence his quick departure. "Ah, Jane" I said, "your jeans, here they are". She looked at me and said that she had something to tell me. She reached into the back pocket of her jeans and pulled out a small ball of silver foil, I said, "what is that?", she informed me that it was cannabis, which she got from the Bedouin. I took a deep breath and asked her to leave my room. She then said that if the border guard had found it, she would have owned up. I looked up at her and said that it would not have helped me, as I would have ended up in jail with her, but she was not convinced. Again, I asked her to leave my room.

I was proud of myself that day, as I managed to remain calm under the circumstances. The next day I was getting ready to go to the local ringing station to do some birding, when Jane asked if she could come with me, of course I was delighted regardless of what had happened. On arriving at the reserve, I introduced myself to one of the ringers there who happened to be German. I took the opportunity to speak to him in German as it's my way of keeping my hand in. I asked the guy if he had caught any Dead Sea Sparrows in his nets. He said he had not, but if he catches one, he would bring it over to show us. Sometime later, we were watching a Pied Kingfisher hovering and diving into the water for fish, when I saw the German guy heading our way with a cloth bag in his hand. I said to Jane, "it looks like he is bringing a Dead Sea Sparrow for us to see", Jane replied "why would I want to see a Dead, Sea-sparrow". I laughed and explained that it's not dead; that's its name because of where it lives, the Dead Sea. She then realised what she had said and laughed as well. She felt slightly embarrassed, although she had no need to be; if you do not know, then you do not know. This sparrow used to breed in Cyprus but sadly it doesn't any more. I once visited a former limestick-trapper turned conservationist in Nicosia. He told me about a time he was having lunch with a high-powered government official to discuss the protection of birds in Cyprus by banning liming and as they were sitting down for their meal, he saw that they had pickled Tree Pipit on the menu. He told me that he ended the meeting there and then.

In 1981 I joined 27th Field R. A. One day I was working in the MT (Motor Transport) office when one of the guys asked me what my interests were. When I told him I was a birdwatcher, he replied "only gay people watch birds". My response was to invite him to close the office door so we could rearrange the furniture, but he declined my offer. Perhaps I could have been a bit more diplomatic and asked him what gave him the right to steal my oxygen. Leaping forward to when I was a Sergeant in 49th Regiment R. A.

I had become well known for my interest in birding and conservation. One day when the regiment was on parade, the Colonel came up to me during his inspection of the men and said, "Sergeant McMullan, the Brigadier wants to have a conservation day soon. I would like you to come up with something. You have the whole regiment at your disposal". I chuckled, the Colonel looked at me and said, "I'm sorry did I say something funny?" I apologised and said, "I was just reflecting back to when I was eighteen Sir, on this very gun park, I was accused of being gay because I watch birds". Putting on a bit of a camp voice, I went on to say, hey ho, how times have changed. I am not sure he saw the funny side of it.

While working for a rehab in Marbella, I decided that I would spend a night up in the mountains. I got dropped off in the morning and spent the day watching warblers all over the place, a Short-toed Eagle was resting nearby, and I glimpsed a large unidentified eagle soaring away from me in the distance. As the light began to fade, I was walking along a large track looking for somewhere to pitch for the night, when within inches of my right ear a Red-necked Nightjar flew past me and landed in the middle of the track a short distance in front of me. Considering nightjars are not that easy to see, this chap presented me with a great view. I eventually decided on a place to sleep for the night, it was on top of a small concrete construction which supplied water to the surrounding olive groves, as I settled down for the night, I could hear Wild Boar moving around high up in the hills behind me.

I lay there listening to the night sounds, when I became aware that the boars were getting closer and it sounded like there was quite a lot of them as well. As they continued to get closer, it slowly dawned on me that they might be heading my way to get their first drink of the night. The construction I was intending to sleep on was pouring water out at a continuous rate. Thinking to myself, perhaps it is not a good idea to sleep here after all, as I could find myself surrounded by a sounder of Wild Boar. Based on my experiences with them in Germany I learnt to give them lots of respect, because if you don't, a single boar can be tough to deal with, let alone a herd of them. I decided to head off down the mountain trail just to be on the safe side. I eventually found a place where it felt safe to spend the night in amongst some rocks.

It was a cold night and sleep was sporadic at best, suddenly I became aware that something was close by, I opened my eyes and there looking at me from behind a boulder was a Fox, breathing a sigh of relief I exchanged greetings with him before, he moved off, he looked like a young male who seemed curious to find out what I was, then I remembered that I had purchased some fresh meat earlier in the day, which had a strong smell to it and as such I was going to attract the attention of animals from miles around.

The rest of the night was uneventful apart from the loss of sleep, as dawn came, I decided, to take a slow walk down the mountain, I could see Marbella in the distance. Along the way I encountered a beautiful Lesser Kestrel doing the most amazing dance with the wind, it was flying very close to the rock face. The pure skill and mastery this bird showed was out of this world, you could see he was clearly in tune with his surroundings, he knew every nook and cranny on the rockface, and he used it to show off his skill of flying.

I was returning to the gun position having just picked up some ammunition, I looked out the window of my truck, just as a coyote ran past our vehicle, we were traveling at 30mph. In hot pursuit of the coyote was what could only be described as one of the Hounds of the Baskervilles. It was a large dog almost Doberman like, its head was massive, in relation to its body and I swear to you, it had bright red eyes. I said to Geordie my driver, look at that coyote, it is running for its F%@king life, and that dog has only one thing in mind and that is to have it for lunch. As they passed our truck the coyote changed direction, deciding to cross the track in front of our vehicle and in so doing it lost some of its traction. Like the cartoon characters in Road Runner, its back legs were going ten to the dozen as the hound snapped at its back legs. Once again, the coyote changed direction and headed up hill parallel to the track we were on, then it disappeared over the hill, with the Baskerville inches away from its tail.

A short time later we saw the hound on its way back heading in the direction it had come from, he was looking well pleased with himself. I got to wondering how on earth this dog ended up here on the prairie. I did some research and found that a lot of dogs had been released by the Black Foot Nation when they went onto the reservations.

I guess this big black hound may have been one of the descendants from that time. That day I will never forget, even from the safety of our cab, with both doors locked.

Whilst driving back to base, I saw in the distance a sight I never thought I would ever see in my lifetime: a pack of Wolves, resting. There was no hint of a reintroduction programme taking place but there was a programme for deer from the Banff and the Jasper areas to be reintroduced as a herd back onto the prairie, so it makes sense to have an apex predator not only to check the deer population but also to reduce and check the coyote population as well. My guess is that the authorities would not want to make it public that wolves were there, given the hostility some people would feel towards their presence.

I was given the task of setting up an ambush for a leadership course with my men. We set out for the location we were given and told to ambush the patrol that will come down the track at five in the morning. We arrived at three in the morning, having recced the location prior to setting up the ambush I knew where I wanted it to be. I got some of the boys to work setting out trip wires that would set off flares, which would light up the area for us, the rest of the patrol set about settling into the hillside looking directly into the killing zone, so to speak. Five o'clock arrived and no patrol, I figured they got delayed, I decided to wait a while longer, six o'clock and still no patrol, that's when I realised they were not coming (I found out later they had got themselves well and truly lost), it was at this point when I was about to give the order to pack up that some Germans arrived in the field below us.

Out of curiosity I watched them and quickly realised that they were hunters preparing to do a shoot. They sent out their beaters to drive the wildlife in their direction, while they waited to take the birds and animals out when they appeared.

My men and I looked at each other, we smiled, and I said to them, "you know what lads, no point in wasting our time, so let's use up all of our ammunition". I gave the order to make ready and they all cocked their weapons, I then ordered them to fire; we all opened up with our guns; we threw thunder flashes which make very load bangs to simulate explosives. Needless to say, the pigeons, rabbits and any other wildlife in the vicinity disappeared in all directions and of course the hunters were very unhappy with us. They were still shaking their fists and shouting at us as we set off down the track back to our vehicles to go back to base. I guess; we upset the hunters. All in all, I think it was a good days hunting.

Left Inset - Left to Right: Patricia Casco, Geoffrey McMullan, Hugo Gonzaalez and Martjan Limmertink. Right Inset: Male Helmeted Woodpecker (HEWO). Below Right Male HEWO. Photo by: Martjan Limmertink.

Left Photo: Martjan with decoy he made. Right Top Photo: Martjan radio tracking a woodpecker. Right Bottom Photo: Geoffrey and Martjan. Photo by: Martjan Limmertink.

Main Photo: Me with the near threatened Yellow-browed Woodpecker. Inset Photo: Me with the vulnerable Helmeted Woodpecker. Photo by: Martjan Limmertink.

Top Left and Middle Photo: White-throated woodpecker at nest hole. Top Right and Bottom Left and Right Photo: The vulnerable Kaempfer's Woodpecker. Photos by Tulio Dornas.

Top Left and Right Photo: The Critically Endangered Endemic
Okinawan woodpecker. Photos by Lynne Millard. Bottom Left and
Right Photo: Strickland's Woodpecker. Photos by Brian Stech.

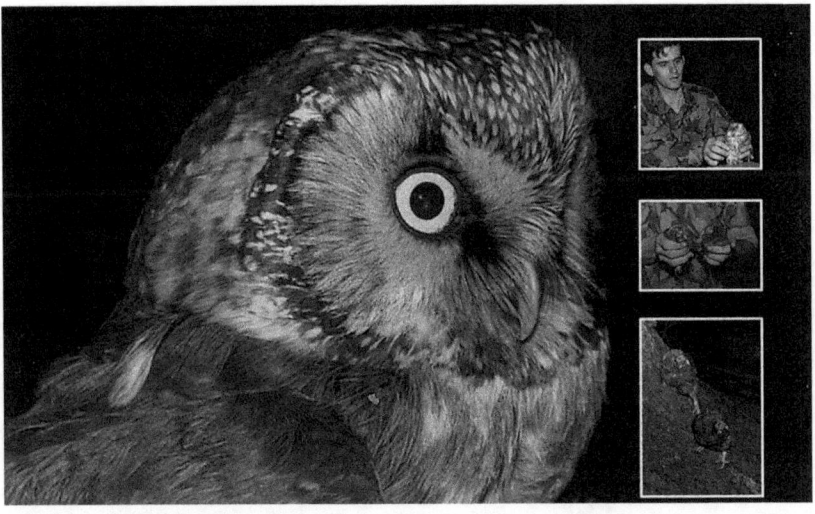

Me with Tengmalm's or Boreal Owls. Photos by Andreas Kampfer

Egyptian Nightjar, AOS trip to Morocco. Photos by Tim Cowley.

The Near Threatened Magellanic Penguin and King
Penguin. Photos by Geoffrey McMullan.

Top Left to Right: South Georgia, me at the museum. Bottom Left to Right: Ernest Shackleton's grave, Weddell Seal, Felix Artuso grave. Photos by Geoffrey McMullan.

Top Left to Right: Carlota a Turquoise-fronted Amazon Parrot helping herself to food off my plate, Rufous-chested Dotterel. Bottom Left to Right: Mountain Chickadee, Spotted Flycatcher, Wandering Albatross, Black-browed Albatross. Photos by Geoffrey McMullan.

Top Clockwise: Inset: Skua attack, Striated Caracara, Dark-faced
Ground Tyrant, Long-tailed Meadowlark, South American Snipe,
White-tufted Grebe. Photos by Geoffrey McMullan.

Top Left to Right: Horseback Birding Costa Rica, Barn Swallow and
Striated Caracara Kidney Island, Falklands. Bottom left to right: Chilean
Flamingo on Pebble Island, Falklands. Egyptian Plover, Gambia.
Wilson's Storm Petrel on board the Grey Rover, South Georgia.

Top Left to Right: Me birding on Islay, and in search of Flamingos in Belize.
Bottom Left to Right: Me cutting through Red Mangroves in Belize, trapping
Sand Martins, lighting a tinder bundle for my fire, outside my cave on Islay.

Top Left to Right: First round away in the counter bombardment exercise, and first
round landing from the return fire. Bottom Left to Right: That one landed a bit close,
and 1st Gulf War, M109 moving to our next location. Photos by Geoffrey McMullan.

Looking at the sun at 10:00hrs through a sky full of oil, Oil fires,
Driving through 'Bomb Alley'. Photos by Geoffrey McMullan.

Bosnia. Top Left to Right: AS90 and driving to resupply one of our rebroadcast
stations. Bottom Left to Right: The final resting place for the people found
under the bridge, Iain Wilkie looking on at the mass grave. Ken Barma, myself
and Nick Hook finding time to relax. Photos by Geoffrey McMullan.

Photos Clockwise: AOS trips to Morocco. The Gambian River Bird Survey Team in Senegal. CAOS trip to the Zachariassee in Germany. The Gambian River and Morocco.

Top Left to Right: Payara - aka the Vampire Fish and Maya Village near to Punta Gorda Belize. Bottom Left to Right: Refuelling an RAF Tornado in the Falklands, writing down the Blackstart I had just seen in the Sinai Desert, Tikal the Snake Temple in Guatemala, and the team and I that went looking for the flamingos in Belize. Photos by Geoffrey McMullan.

Top Left to Right: Iguazú Falls the largest waterfall system in the world, Kaieteur Falls is the world's largest single drop waterfall by the volume of water flowing over it. Bottom: The Temples of Tikal, bathing time near the edge of the Kaieteur Falls. Photos by Geoffrey McMullan.

Various Shelters I have lived in over the years. Bottom Left: Me with Merlin.

Zachariassee Nature Reserve. Insets Peter Hoffmann, Freshwater Jellyfish,
Breeding Oystercatcher, hide. Photos by Peter Hoffmann.

Zachariassee. Photos Top: Bittern, Black Tern in winter plumage, Oystercatcher,
Grey Plover Common Sandpiper. Bottom: Left Inset: Marsh Harrier. Right
Inset Cranes. Main Photo Cranes at the Zach. Photos by Peter Hoffman.

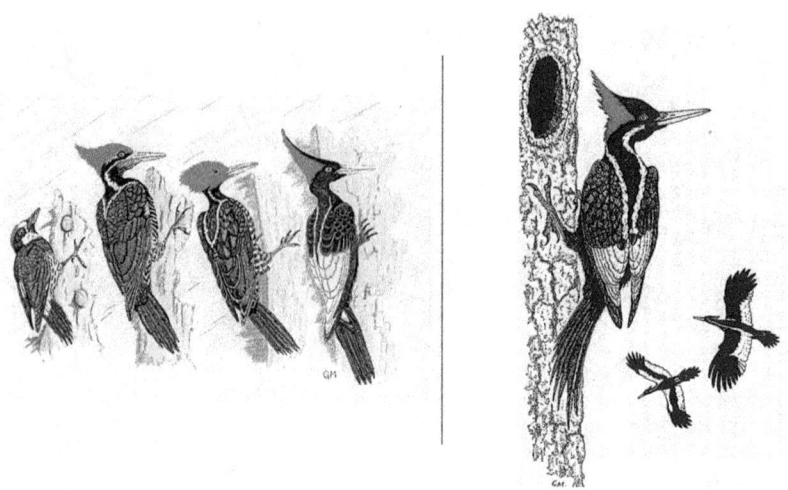

Drawings I did for Martjan for the Cuban Ivory-billed
Woodpecker and the Imperial Woodpecker.

CHAPTER 5

Bandit Country vs Falklands

Bandit Country or the Falklands? I had a choice. My first option was six months in the winter, being shot at from across the border in South Armagh, which is known as 'Bandit Country' to the British Soldier. Bandit Country is around two hundred square miles of the most dangerous and hostile terrain in Northern Ireland which has claimed the lives of many British Soldiers since 1969. To the republicans, it is 'God's Country' and the only area in the six counties where the so-called occupiers were perhaps 'successfully' resisted.

My second option was the Falklands, a windswept archipelago located three hundred miles off the coast of Argentina in the ice-cold waters of the South Atlantic. Spending four months in the summer, where nearly every bird would be a lifer, where orcas patrol the coastal waters, albatrosses sail the winds with ease, and dolphins abound. It really was a no-brainer.

My journey began while I served with 49th Regiment R. A. The regiment was being disbanded because of cutbacks and phase two redundancies were offered to many of the guys. It is fair to say, those that were offered it, took the money and ran. We all thought it was crazy to disband our regiment as it was a great regiment to be in. It was decided that 127 (Dragon) Battery, would join 26th Regiment R. A. in a town called Gütersloh; which was 31kms to the north of Lippstadt and interestingly that is where I started out on my first posting.

Once the decision had been made, the powers to be set about deciding who should go where and in some cases, people wanted to be posted to other units in Germany or the United Kingdom. Some personnel were moved from other Battery's within the regiment to ours in order to bolster our numbers and to ensure that we got the best people from within the regiment. As the Motor Transport Sergeant (MT Sgt) I was responsible for the transportation of vehicles and equipment to our new camp.

We set off to Gütersloh and began the process of getting our equipment in place which had to be combat ready within a given period of time. I went on to become the Regimental Fleet Manager (RFM) as a Sergeant in a Staff Sergeant's (S/Sgt's) post. One day we received an order to parade on the hockey pitch; this was an open tarmacked area next to the gym. The hockey pitch was also used to warn the residing regiment off for operational tours, and it was no different now. As the regiment paraded, we waited for the 'old man' CO to arrive, speculation was rife amongst the guys. The Colonel eventually arrived in his staff car, he then proceeded to tell the regiment that we were officially 'warned off' for a six-month operational tour in South Armagh.

I was very happy with this, not because it was six months in 'bandit country', on an operational tour known as 'Op Banner'; but because as a Belfast Boy, I saw it as going home albeit in uniform. I had no doubt that I could wangle some time off to visit my family over in Belfast and Bangor. After the euphoria of going home had settled, I went about my normal duties. A few days later, I was on my NAAFI break (The Navy, Army and Air Force Institutes) in the canteen when my Troop Sergeant Major (TSM) came looking for me. Having found me, he pulled up a chair; sitting in silence he looked at me with a big grin on his face. I looked up from eating my NAAFI pie and asked him what he wanted, he said "I have just got rid of another Sergeant (Sgt) from my troop". I looked at him blankly and enquired what on earth he was talking about. He said "I have been on a mission to get all of the senior Dragons out of my troop and replace them with seniors from Thombs troop (Thombs was his Bty from our disbanded regiment).

He went on to inform me that there is one last Sgt to get rid of, and while he was staring straight at me, he went silent again. I responded by saying "I take it you mean me"; continuing to smile, he said "yes". I have to say I admired his nerve. One for interrupting me during my break, which was precious to me and two for his honesty, even though he had a negative intent towards me. I leaned back in my chair, looked him in the eye, and said, "you had better shoot straight as I do not go down easily" and with that, he got up and left the canteen. I carried on with my meal thinking to myself, cheeky F@%&er. It was about a week later when I received a phone call in my office. I immediately recognised his voice. "Hello Sir" I said. He opened the conversation with, "how would you like an all-expenses paid trip to the Falkland Islands?

I replied, "is that the best you can do" and hung up on him. That evening, in my room I began to think about the events of the day and slowly but surely it began to dawn on me. In my head I was saying to myself, hang on Geoffrey think about it; six months, bandit country or four months in the Falklands. Which is somewhere I have never been before with loads of wildlife and maybe I can fix it so I can travel back via South America. The next morning, I called the TSM and I asked him if the posting to the Falkland's was still going. He said, "do you want it?". I said "yes", he replied "done, it's yours". The posting gave me the Acting Rank of S/Sgt which meant I would be paid as a S/Sgt for four months while holding a Sergeants Rank.

A few months later I was winging my way down to the Falklands, flying out of Brize Norton on a Royal Air Force Tri-Star for my first tour and some serious birding. The RAF give their aircraft names, for example a passenger Tri-Star is known as a Timmy, while a cargo Tri-Star is a Tommy and a C130 Hercules is called a Fat Albert, I have no idea why. However, one of their Tri-Star's was also named Damien and it lived up to its name, as it would always breakdown at the most inconvenient times, or was it really 'inconvenient'?

In the army we have something that is known as a 'tactical breakdown'. This occurs because the crew of a given vehicle have decided that they want to have a rest from an exercise, so they might deliberately sabotage their vehicle in order to drop out of the exercise. We had a short stopover on Ascension Island to refuel and rest a bit before carrying on to the Falklands. Prior to entering the terminal, an American soldier met us, he informed us that we did not see a piece of military hardware that was parked just beyond our Tri-Star. Up until then no one had seen it and of course some of the guys saw this as an opportunity to have fun with him by saying things like "you mean the

S&%@*#h plane parked over there?". The American was taking his job seriously and he became frustrated with our banter. I am not able to tell you what we saw due to a commitment that I made, which I still must abide by, namely the Official Secrets Act.

As we approached the Falkland Islands, I was looking out of the window enjoying the cloudless blue sky, when we were joined by two Tornados. One on the port wing, and the other was off the starboard wing, it is normal practice for incoming aircraft to have a fighter escort. It served as a reminder that the Islands were always on a state of combat readiness.

Debussing (Disembarking) from the Timmy, I made my mark straight away. There was a warrant officer stood at the entrance to the air terminal, I acknowledged his presence by greeting him with the words, 'Hello Sir'. "SIR?", "it's Madam to you" she bellowed back at me. I thought oh s@%t as I realised that he was a she. The person I was addressing was the Senior Warrant Officer (SWO) in the army this equates to a Regimental Sergeant Major (RSM). I soon got to know her, not only was she a very kind person towards me during a period of personal difficulty in my married life (and I am grateful to her for that), but she was also a birdwatcher and my office was one down from hers. After settling into my room, I looked out of my bedroom window and bagged a Long-tailed Meadowlark, which is an endemic also known as the Military Starling. This is because of its bright red chest, which is reminiscent of the red tunics worn by the Guards at Buckingham Palace. It was the first of what was to be a long list of lifers.

I decided to take a wander to get a feel for the place. My room and office were within a major complex which contained the world's longest corridor measuring half a mile (800m) nicknamed the 'Death Star Corridor', perhaps because of its forced air system, which is great for spreading germs.

I met with Joe, the guy who I was replacing; he took me out to for a walk so that I could get my bearings, one of the first places we headed for, was Bertha's Beach which has a long, white sandy beach stretching for as far as the eye can see. It was bordered by extensive coastal dunes, large freshwater ponds and brackish lagoons on one side and a vast blue fresh smelling ocean on the other. I did not have to wait long before I had my second lifer and not just an Island lifer, but a mega lifer, my first from the South American mainland. It was a Least Seedsnipe, there have been many sightings of this bird on the islands since 1926, breeding has long been suspected; I saw mine on the 27th November 1993. It was a male, calling from a small earth mound, and the backdrop was one of the Royal Navy's, Type 42 Destroyers, a grand ship and a grand crew.

I was congratulating myself on choosing the Falklands over 'Bandit Country', as a birder the Falklands was heaven, and every spare moment I had was spent birding. In fact after sorting out my office and getting the feel for my new job the only time I would be in my office on a weekend was not to catch up with work but to put myself ahead of the things I had been tasked with, just so I could get more birding in.

On my return from a day's birding I found this picture taped to my bedroom door, I have no idea who put it there, but I did laugh. ▶

My favourite place was without doubt Kidney Island; so, called due to its shape, it's a small island of 33 hectares (82 acres). Kidney is a nature reserve and unlike most of the main islands it is covered in Tussac Grass, which is a species native to southern South America and the Falkland Islands.

Tussac usually grows to about 2m high (although they can be much taller). I am six foot four inches (195 cm) and I have experienced Tussac almost twice my height. Some of the birds on the Island include Rockhopper Penguins, Imperial Shags, and Sooty Shearwaters in their thousands. The Island is one of three places in the archipelago where King Penguins breed; the other places are Saunders Island and Volunteer Point on the East of the Falklands. There is a small wooden cabin located on one side of the island. On one of my trips there I was with some of my RAF friends. They were a great bunch of guys but I kind of saw them as 'civvies' (civilian's) in uniform; when I told them this, they pointed out that the RAF send their officers to war by plane, the Navy go to sea with their officers but in the Army the officers send the lower ranks to war, while they stay behind in the hotels. Of course, this is just banter; inter-force rivalry is a healthy thing; it adds to the spice of life. One evening while I was standing outside of the cabin, I was greeted by two Short-eared Owls circling overhead, what a magnificent sight that was. However, nothing prepared me for what I was about to encounter, I took a walk across the island and ended up on a rocky outcrop.

Looking out to sea, I saw hundreds, literally hundreds of Sooty Shearwaters rafting just offshore. As dusk fell, they started to take flight, swarming before moving towards where I was standing. They dropped lower and lower; some were flying so close to me that I felt dizzy at times. I almost lost my balance as one passed within centimetres of my right ear. Suddenly they started dropping like stones all around me and once on the ground, they scurried off into the Tussac. While they looked clumsy on the ground, they could move very fast in their efforts to get into their burrows. As I walked back to the hut, I looked up and spread across the night sky was a stunning view of the Milky Way.

The next day we went for a walk along the shoreline, Angus went up ahead to take a leak (urinate) in amongst the Tussac. As we passed the point where he had disappeared, he was nowhere to be seen. Clearly, he was the shy type and had gone deeper into the grass. Suddenly, we heard screaming coming from behind us, we turned just as Angus came running out of the Tussac, improperly dressed I might add; by that I mean his manhood was hanging out and flapping all over the place. It was understandable when you consider that hot on his heels was the biggest Bull Fur Seal you could ever wish to see in your life. This fella was so big he commanded respect, as he was well over six feet tall. Separated by the Bull; we on one side and Angus on the other. This guy only had to flinch, nay blink and we would run. It is always best not to underestimate seals. They may look big and cumbersome but when they want to, they really can move. After a while the seal decided we were not worth bothering about, and he made his way into the sea, and we headed off towards the hut. As we headed back, I was jumping from one rock to the next along the shoreline when I had the fright of my life as I jumped onto a large boulder, it suddenly moved. I soon realised that one side of the boulder was a head and the other was a tail, both were arching their way up towards me. It was a young Elephant Seal, thankfully I was off it in a jiffy and it did not give chase. For a small island there was plenty to see. From, the endemic Cobb's Wren, and the Tussac-bird (also known as Blackish Cinclodes), to the Kelp Goose. I travelled to Kidney Island three times during my tour; I enjoyed the solitude it offered; I would pop down into Port Stanley and hire one of the locals to take me out on their boat.

The Falkland's was a place where you could do a lot or just do nothing other than drink. I particularly enjoyed my relationship with the C130 Hercules Squadron. One day I managed to hitch a ride on a mission to refuel our Tornado Jets. We were flying over Bird Island South Georgia; when I threw up, I was sick no less than four times due to the smell of the aviation fuel. My RAF buddies found it amusing, but I am sure it was not the first time they witnessed such a scene on a refuelling mission.

There were many stories floating around the Falkland's; from an Iceberg the size of Wales heading our way, to a penguin falling over backwards as it watched a helicopter fly directly overhead. I suspect that these were probably April Fools jokes.

After the war, British troops noticed similarities between the Islanders and that of a character named Benny from an old TV soap called 'Crossroads'. Benny was a less than academically gifted odd job man, known for wearing old knitted jumpers and a woolly hat. It seems that some soldiers started calling the Islanders 'Bennies', and when the Islanders found out they complained to the Governor who in turn reported it to the Station Commander, and he was asked to put a stop to it. The order was given that if any service personal were caught referring to the islanders as Benny's they would be disciplined. The story I had heard was that shortly after the ban the Station Commander was being driven into Port Stanley one day, and as they turned onto the main road his driver said," oh look Sir, there's a Still". The Commander asked, "what's a Still?". His driver replied, "they're still F&%king Bennies".

In fairness the islanders called us 'Whennies', because, when soldiers tell their stories, they would often start them with "When I was in the Falklands..." or "When I was in Bosnia..." etc.

I often went on a 'Bimble' (trip out). This expression is believed to have originated amongst British Soldiers serving in the Falklands. On one occasion John the chief clerk and I had planned to head out to Kidney Island however, the weather closed in on us and we had to cancel the trip, instead we headed for Cape Pembroke Lighthouse which was not far from Port Stanley. On the way we had a close encounter with a juvenile Red-backed Hawk, we stopped for a while to take pictures.

Driving on the road to Stanley could at times be dangerous; it is around 48.5 kilometres (30.2 miles) from RAF Mount Pleasant (MPA); within Stanley the roads are asphalted; all other roads however were gravelled all-weather roads. You had to watch your speed as you could end up aquaplaning on the gravel.

We arrived at the lighthouse having driven about a mile off the main drag (road). The lighthouse has a stone bench facing out to sea, which was surrounded by a half circle stonewall, which afforded us some shelter from the wind. It was an ideal spot for setting up our scopes, we unpacked our Haverdog's, (lunchboxes) broke open our flasks for a brew and settled into an awe-inspiring experience of wall to wall seabirds passing from right to left as we watched them through our scopes, sometimes there would be birds going in the other direction. The wind was strong, and the birds were so close it made for fantastic birding.

Black-browed Albatross were plentiful, as were Cape Petrels, Southern Giant Petrels, Kelp Gulls, Blue Petrels and Southern Fulmars. We lost track of time even though it was very cold with a strong wind. Then it started to rain; we carried on birding for a while longer unaware of the flooding taking place behind us.

We decided it was time to leave and that's when we realised that the ground was like a swamp. I said to John, "are you up for a rough ride?" he said that he was. The ten-minute drive from the road took us some 20-30 minutes to get back. It involved driving up onto high ground, sometimes slamming the vehicle immediately into reverse and taking a different route to avoid getting bogged in. We went up, down, backwards, forwards and often the rear end would slide on the wet slippery surface, almost sending us into a spin.

We stopped for short periods to assess the situation, sometimes carrying out a foot recce of the lay of the land in order to find the safest route out. With tired aching muscles, I really had to work hard, it was perhaps the hardest I had ever worked driving a Land Rover off-road. The whole time John was hanging on, bracing himself between the doorframe, his seat and the dashboard; I asked if he was ok. He replied, "I am great, and this is awesome!" I could see by his face, that he was excited by the experience. He paid me a compliment by saying that it was the best bit of off-road driving he had ever seen. For my part, my backside had amazing suction power on my seat, my seatbelt was off as it was restricting my movement and my knuckles were white from gripping onto the steering wheel. I was relieved when we hit the metal road (normal tarmac). On our way back to MPA we were just entering Port Stanley, when we saw a Flying Steamer Duck the only one I saw during both tours.

The fun did not stop as we ended up with a puncture; thank goodness the weather had cleared by then. I attempted to find level ground, but this proved to be difficult without causing damage to the vehicle, so I decided to attempt to change the wheel on a steep gradient. Fortunately, we had two jacks. With handbrake on, vehicle in gear and the wheels chocked I used one jack to support the vehicle using the slope of the road to act as a brace. John's job was to make sure I was safe, as it involved going under the vehicle a short distance using the other to jack lift up the rear axle.

John stood directly behind me and I gave him the instruction that if the vehicle showed any sign of coming off the jack, he was to drag me out from underneath it. His hands were gripping my lapels in preparation, but I am pleased to say it did not come to that and we returned to MPA safe and sound.

The next day I spotted a large white bird landing in a ditch outside my office window, grabbing my bins I saw that it was a Snowy Egret which was my second mainland rarity. Later that night, I was laying on my bed reflecting on the birds I had seen so far, while watching the moon rise in the left-hand corner of my bedroom window, I was taken aback by the speed with which the moon traversed the night sky. In no time at all it had vanished from my view. I had never seen the moon pass by so quickly. As I said before, my days off were spent getting out and about as much as I could, be it on foot, in a vehicle, by boat or in a helicopter to one of the offshore islands such as Sea Lion Island. I arranged a trip to Sea Lion to help a local farmer with his lambs and of course to bird the Island. To get around from island to island, people used the Falkland Islands Government Air Service, (FIGAS). The planes held eight to ten people and landed on airstrips that were nothing more than grassy fields. The seats on the planes were so small that I could not find any degree of comfort. If you were lucky, the pilot would let you sit in the co-pilot's seat, where there was some leg room. I was really looking forward to seeing the five species of penguin, and Striated Caracara; also known as Johnny Rook and considered one of the most intelligent of all the worlds birds of prey. The Falklands holds the world's largest population of Striated Caracara.

On this occasion I arrived by Chinook helicopter and immediately on landing, the owner of the hotel near to the landing site rushed out and charged everyone £3 as a landing fee. I later found out he had no right to do this. Arriving at the shepherd's house I saw my first House Sparrow since being in the Falklands. Wherever I go in the world the ubiquity of the House Sparrow never ceases to amaze me. It's intentional or accidental introduction to many regions of the world, make it the most widely distributed wild bird. I also bagged a rare and accidental Rufous-collared Sparrow sitting on the garden fence; this was now my third mainland species.

The deal with the farmer and his wife was they would give me food and board in exchange for doing something that remotely looked like working hard, although I have to say that ringing lamb's tails was indeed hard work. On my days off from lambing, I would go for a walk to see the penguins and other wildlife. In the distance I spotted a large group of people looking out to sea, I thought, hello they have found something interesting. I quickly made my way over only to find out I had just dipped out on seeing my first ever pod of Killer Whales. It would have been so cool to see them, I guess that's for another day. I carried on with my walk; there were plenty of Gentoo Penguins around, and boy did they smell. I also started to notice a lot of Skua carcasses lying around with shotgun cartridges nearby. Further along I had some great views of Johnny Rook, one of which came close to me while I was sitting down. Johnny Rook is primarily a scavenger feeding on carrion (mainly dead seabirds) and scraps of food.

A short while later I met the Station Commander (SC); we got chatting about the birds he had seen as he was a keen birdwatcher himself. I pointed out to him that I had seen a lot of dead Skua's with shotgun cartridges nearby. The SC said that he had been talking with the owner from the hotel who had told him that he was shooting the Skua's because they were killing off the baby penguins and upsetting the balance of nature, which in turn was upsetting the tourists. I suspect he was more concerned with the loss of revenue to his hotel; perhaps fearing that the tourists would not come back because of Skua's eating young penguins.

While killing Skua's was not illegal he was leaving the carcasses with shotgun pellets inside them. My concern was that Johnny Rook would scavenge on the carcasses and in turn they would ingest the pellets. If these were lead shot, which I believed them to be, then Johnny Rook could be indirectly poisoned. Given that it is a rare and endangered species, it is of course protected. On my return to camp I decided that I would write a letter of complaint to the local authorities in which I included the comments made by the SC without actually naming him. I recorded my own observations in the letter, and I requested that all of the carcasses be removed in order to avoid any indirect poisoning of Johnny Rook. About a week later, my boss stormed into my office demanding to know why I had reported the guy on Sea Lion Island, as she frantically waved a copy of my letter in front of my face. She then said that I had no right to report him and that she would take this matter directly to the SC. I tried to let her know that the third-party mentioned in my letter, was in fact the SC as I did not want her to embarrass herself, but she ignored my pleas for her to listen, and off she went. A few hours later the SC's personal assistant (PA) came into my office to inform me of what had happened. It seems that my boss really went on one and she had demanded that I be removed from my position.

The SC asked to see the letter and according to his PA, having read it he handed it back to her and said that it was the correct account of events and he informed her that he was in fact the third party and he agreed with my assessment. According to the SC's PA, my boss was stunned into silence. She did not return to my office to inform me of the outcome, I had to go to her office to ask her if there was any feedback for me. She gave my letter and said I could go ahead and send it, which confused me somewhat as I had already sent it. I felt this was a small or maybe even a large victory won on behalf of Johnny Rook. Sometimes you just have to upset the apple cart if you want things to change.

I had an opportunity to go birding by boat with one of the local birders from Stanley. We went to explore some of the inlets and as we crossed the harbour to get to our destination, we were given a wonderful display of a Peale's Dolphin breaching; which is a small endemic dolphin. This was the first time I had ever seen a dolphin breaching. Peale's are often found in areas of fast-moving waters, such as entrances to channels as well as close to the shore or in safe areas such as bays. As we travelled up one of the channels, directly in front of us we saw a small group of Peale's Dolphins. I was at the front of the boat taking pictures of them when I realised that they were driving a school of fish onto a bank in order to catch and eat them; I became very excited to be a witness to this rare event.

I remember watching Sir David Attenborough talking about a species of dolphin in Africa being the only dolphin that behaves like this. I am not saying that I had discovered something new in dolphin behaviour but more likely that this behaviour had gone unreported in other species of dolphins. I was clicking away with my camera, feeling excited about seeing the photographs and how they would come out when suddenly my camera jammed.

Try as I might I could not free it and reluctantly I was forced to open the camera thus exposing the film. I guess this was another one of those moments in life where it was not necessary to take pictures, just as it was with the Whimbrel on Islay. We continued the rest of the morning looking for birds; we managed to see Upland Geese, Austral Thrush, Crested Caracaras, and Crested Ducks. Out in the lagoons we also saw White-tufted Grebes and a Black-necked Swans.

By now John and I were doing regular birding trips and our next trip was to Bertha's beach. Arriving at the beach we saw literally hundreds of White-rump Sandpipers., they were wall to wall and amongst them we were able to pick out a single Baird's Sandpiper; without doubt the bird of the trip. These little fellas had travelled all the way from their breeding grounds in the northern tundra of Western Greenland and when you think about the distance, which can be up to 2600 miles, it is quite an amazing feat given their size (7-7.6 in / 180-190 mm). Bertha's Beach is beautiful with an abundance of bird and marine life. Commerson's Dolphins were a regular feature at the beach, often coming close to the shore as they played in the shallows and surfed the waves. The birds were not fazed by our presence, allowing us to get close to them, especially the Black-throated Finches.

We continued our walk along the beach; Magellanic and Blackish Oystercatchers were in abundance, as were Kelp Geese and Two-banded Plovers. We climbed over a rocky outcrop and continued along the beach, when I spotted some Commerson's Dolphins. I told John that I was going in to swim with them. John who was filming at the time, looked up from his camera and said, "you must be mad, the water must be bloody freezing", I responded saying that this might be a once-in-a-lifetime opportunity. In I went. I got as close as they would allow, and I reckon that I spent a good 10 minutes in the water before I had to leave because it was so cold. Later on, I watched the film that John had taken of me in the surf with the dolphins. He was doing a running commentary and it went like this: "This is Geoff, he is in the artillery and clearly he has been hit by a very large shell because any sane person would not even consider going into the sea. It's so freezing cold even the locals do not go in".

The SWO called me into her office. She informed me that an Argentinian, body had been pushed up from under the peat on Pebble Island. The plan was to repatriate him back to Argentina, in order to do this, we had to fly him by Hercules to Montevideo and hand over the body to the Argentines, the SWO tasked me to carry this out. Sadly, the Argentine authorities did not want the body back, instead they wanted it to be left there. I really felt for the families of the deceased soldier because they were denied closure and a proper burial for their loved one.

There are not many birdwatchers in the Falklands that said, word still gets around when something new and unusual turns up. One day, I received word that a Chilean Flamingo had turned up on Pebble Island, so my next mission was to organise a flight over there. While there, I stayed with one of the locals and the lady of the house baked some excellent bread to go with the most amazing homemade soup. It has to be said that during my two tours of the Falkland's I found the locals (apart from one, the expat on Sea Lion Island) to be very warm and friendly people.

The next morning, I went, to find the Flamingo and it did not take long to locate it. This was now my fourth mainland species and without question it was quite a beautiful sight to behold. With its outstretched neck and its legs reaching out behind it, this beautiful rosy pink bird took off and flew past me. I never thought I would get excited about a Flamingo, but to see it on Pebble Island was quite something and I even managed to take a photograph of it in flight. I carried on with my walk, stopping to check out a Dark-faced Ground Tyrant, which was standing on a rock with its back to me. It was giving me that sideways look that birds tend to do when they are watching you. Behind the Tyrant I spotted a large white bird; it was swimming in close to the shoreline. As I got closer, I was able to identify it as a Coscoroba Swan and amazingly I was now on my fifth mainland lifer. The Coscoroba Swan breeds in Southern Chile and Central Argentina south to Tierra del Fuego, there has been a breeding record in the Falkland Islands. The Coscoroba is considered an early ancestor to the true geese and swans of today. Many years later I would see these birds again in the Chaco in Paraguay.

A few days after returning from Pebble Island I was in my office, looking through my field guide, when the SWO's aide came in. She looked down at my book and pointed to a bird and said that the SWO and her had seen this bird that day at Fitzroy. I looked up at her and asked, "are you absolutely sure you saw this bird?", she replied, "yes". I immediately got out of my chair and went to the SWO's office. "Ma'am" I said, "I've just been told that you saw this bird at Fitzroy", showing her my field guide and pointing to the bird in question, "is this correct?" I asked. She looked up and said "yes, it is". With no thought to rank, I said to her "get your coat, let's go", "what do you mean?" she asked. I informed her that while there had been sightings of this bird in the Falklands, to date there hadn't been any confirmed sightings and if we could find this bird together it would be the first confirmed sighting. We drove to Fitzroy and Jan, her aide, joined us. We spent a few hours looking around Fitzroy's water edges but to no avail. I had dipped on what would have been my sixth mainland bird. The bird in question was the Magellanic Plover and it is still on my list of birds to see. This bird is a rare and unique wader, found only in the southernmost part of South America. It was placed with other plovers in the family Charadriidae, however research suggests that they are actually more closely related to the Sheathbills which are a uniquely Antarctic family, to the point that it is now placed in its own family, Pluvianellidae.

Sheathbills are not a long-distance migrant, although one did make it to the UK. It was ship assisted courtesy of the Royal Navy, and it was returned to the Falklands, courtesy of Her Majesty's Government at the taxpayers' expense. If I recall correctly the twitchers in the UK went mental.

Once again, I took a boat trip over to Kidney Island to do more exploring, but this time I decided to check out the other side of the island. I trekked uphill through the Tussac Grass, which got taller, bigger and denser the further up I climbed. As the grass got even denser the path also became narrower, to the point where at times I was forced to climb up on top of the grass and step from tussock to tussock. This proved to be very hard work. Eventually a break appeared, and I jumped down; I was making my way through the breaks and to my surprise I encountered a young elephant seal heading downhill. Knowing that this is their territory, I gave way to the seal. He passed by me without incident.

I was really not expecting to see a seal that high up, eventually I reached the top and I could go no further. Across the way was a rocky outcrop which had separated from the rest of the island and from this point I could see hundreds of Imperial Shags. I remember thinking at the time how I could spend the day just leaning against the tussock, enjoying the sun with a fresh breeze coming in from the sea. Just a few feet away from me was a Rockhopper Penguin, this little chap was hanging on the cliff edge by his claws, the only way for him to go, was down, at least 100 feet. I decided to lay down and just spend some quite time with him, as he watched me. Later on, I made my way back down to the beach, the beauty of being on Kidney Island, is there really was no one else around.

As I got to the beach, male Elephant Seals where fighting amongst themselves for breeding rights. I looked around and just offshore I spotted a mass of Rockhoppers porposing through the water, the speed they were moving at was phenomenal. I made my way over to a rocky outcrop just in time to see them turn at a ninety-degree angle without seemly loosing speed. They were heading in my direction. Moments later they were catapulting themselves from the sea landing onto the outcrop; on landing they immediately made their way up the cliff face, one of them was almost at the top when it lost its balance and fell backwards, rolling all the way back to the bottom, only to get up, shake itself off and start again, as if nothing had happened. I was very impressed, if that been me, I would been moaning and groaning before finally picking myself up.

I encountered a Tussac-bird looking for food in and around my boots as I was enjoying my alone time on this wonderful island.

During my first tour of the Falklands I had an opportunity to visit the Ascension Islands, other than the normal stopover to refuel on route to the Falklands. Normally you can only visit the Ascension Islands on R&R if your tour is for six months or you are on your second four-month tour. The reason I was able to visit the islands was because some of my vehicles were there and I needed to inspect them as part of my inventory. I arranged my flight and off I went. I was only there for a weekend and although my time was limited, I did manage to get some birding in. The main bird for me during this time was the Ascension Frigatebird, an endemic to the islands. I also saw a Common Waxbill and a Brown Noddy.

After my first tour of the Falklands I had planned to travel to South America from Port Stanley. Jan, a Navy buddy had arranged for me to join his ship in Valparaíso, Chile. I was excited by this prospect because from Chile the ship was to sail to Easter Island, then to Lima in Peru and from there up to the Galapagos Islands. After spending a few days there, the plan was to then traverse the Panama Canal and onto Jamaica or Trinidad. After which we would then head back to Blighty (UK). Jan came to see me to tell me that the ship was given orders to leave port early; this meant that I would not be able to meet the ship in Chile. Then the news came in that the ship had broken a drive shaft which raised my hopes of joining them again. However, a new shaft was flown down quicker than anticipated so the ship was repaired, and she set sail; still, it was nice to dream about the birds I could have seen. After birding the open sea, I imagined seeing myself sitting in a deck chair with a cold beer on one side, my field guide on the other and my scope between my legs while enjoying the birds of the Panama Canal as we cruised along.

After my first tour, I was back in camp having breakfast in the Sgt's Mess, when Duncan from the Pay Corp mentioned to me that while I was in the Falkland's I would be entitled to four months' worth of Staff Sergeant's pension and gratuity, even if I left as a Sergeant. This got the wheels in my head working overtime, I asked Duncan, "If I leave the army as a Sergeant having completed two years as an acting Staff Sergeant in the Falklands, does that mean I would get a Staff Sergeant's full pension?". He said "yes". I decided that it was now time for a reality check, and to cut a long story short I secured my second posting back to the Falklands; four months after my first tour. The plan was to keep reapplying for an extension while in theatre up to the two-year qualifying period.

During my second tour of the islands I heard that Robin Woods was producing a Breeding Atlas of the birds of the Falkland Islands, so I decided to chance my hand and write to him asking if he needed an illustrator for his book. I was amazed when he replied and that indeed he was looking for an illustrator. He asked me to send in some samples of my work and I must confess that I left it a bit late to send my sample drawings to him, and I felt that they were not of a high enough standard, I thought it would be my own fault if he did not hire me; clearly Robin thought differently, as he awarded me the contract. While I was deployed in Bosnia, I had to adjust some of the drawings. I didn't have any equipment with me, so I had to make the corrections using Tippex and a ballpoint pen (nightmare), it was not ideal, but it had to be done.

On one bimble, Gary, an RAF friend who is also a keen birdwatcher and photographer joined me. Our vehicle was fitted with wide tyres which are known as bimble-tyres which enabled us to cross the rough terrain with ease. The riskiest time was when I drove around the edge of an estuary. The two nearside tyres were hanging onto the solid rock edge and my side was immersed in the water, which also covered half of the windscreen. After emerging from the water, I had to remove the spark plugs to dry them before we could continue with our bimble. Having had a very interesting journey to get to our destination, we parked up to eat some lunch before heading out on foot.

We were heading towards a colony of King Penguins when my attention was drawn to a Brown Skua up on a bank looking straight at me with its wings raised high. It was calling quite aggressively, at first,

I did not pay much attention to its displaying. As I got closer, the Skua decided to attack me, Gary was filming the events as they unfolded.

In the meantime, I was watching the Skua through the lens of my camera. As it flew closer to me, I backed off, but it continued to loom towards me, while I continued to take pictures. The next thing I knew, it had landed on my back. It jumped on and off my back several times until it had forced me to move some distance away from our original encounter.

When I had backed off to a distance it was happy with, it returned to its original spot back on the bank. We decided that it was best to move off, so as not to disturb him any further. We were still unaware of the main reason he attacked me, that is until we passed him, it became very clear why he had; he was protecting his partner and their two chicks; at this point we left them in peace. We then made our way over to a breeding colony of Black-browed Albatrosses. We looked down over the cliff and there before our very eyes were hundreds of young Albatrosses sitting on their mud nests; there was a strong smell of fish in the air. We took it in turns to pose with the young; I got a little bit too close to one of them which spat a strong fish smelling oily fluid in my direction. Thankfully it missed, but boy, it really stank, that smell is something you would not want to get on your clothes that's for sure.

At the end of my second tour I had planned to travel back to Germany via Ascension Island where I would join a ship from Liverpool and sail down to St Helena to bag the Wire-bird, which is an endemic wader to the island. After this I would sail onto Cape Town and travel on up to Zimbabwe. Unfortunately, my boss called me back to help with the handover of our guns (M109's); which had been sold to the Austrians.

At the start of this chapter I mentioned that my TSM wanted rid of me from his troop. It turned out that I did not need to keep reapplying for an extended tour of the Falklands, as nice as that would have been. I was informed during my second tour that I had been promoted to Staff Sergeant. My RAF boss from my first tour had written a glowing confidential report about me and because it was an independent report it could not be blocked by the RSM in my Regiment or anyone else for that matter. I would like to thank my TSM for indirectly facilitating my promotion to Staff Sergeant, and so I returned to Germany to spend what time I could with my children before leaving the Army. In the bag.

CHAPTER 6

Extreme Birding

xtreme birding or as I like to call it sometimes, 'service personnel get to bird where no other birders can'. This is due to the fact that service personnel be they Army, Navy or Air Force can find themselves in extreme situations. They could be training in Canada carrying out live firing exercises or deployed to a conflict zone somewhere in the world. I am sure that extreme birding is not exclusive to members of the armed forces, there must be many birders who have found themselves in extreme situations. Each of the armed forces have their own birding groups, there is the Royal Naval Birdwatching Society (RNBWS), and the Royal Air Force Ornithological Society (RAFOS), and of course the army has the Army Ornithological Society (AOS) with CAOS being the extreme element of the group.

It was always a race between the two Fire Direction Centre's (FDC's) Alpha and Bravo as to who would get into location, set-up and report ready for action first. The loser would be stood-down and be prepared to step-up at any time to take command. This meant that they had to shadow everything that went on over the radios. It was the same with the gun batteries, there was competition to report the first gun ready within each battery, and heavy competition to be the first Battery to report ready within the regiment, and of course the first regiment to report ready.

Thereafter, the FDC's would leapfrog meaning we would take it in turns to move forward or back depending on the state of the battle and taking command of the regiments' fire power once in location. I was on Zero Bravo and I loved it when we were stood down and Zero Alpha was running the show. I also loved being in the box that oversaw the fire power of the regiment (box refers to the AFV 432 the Command Post Variant). I would often do the drag stag which was between the hours of midnight and six in the morning. Many of the guys hated that shift particularly if we had had a tough day, as they just wanted to get their heads down. In my case it had several advantages. I got to wake everyone up in the morning after I had had a wash and shave, and then after breakfast I went to bed. Once I had been promoted to Sgt, I was no longer required to stag-on as a sentry, but I did do radio stags. I would also do the sentry's stag when I 'dropped a bollock' (meaning I had messed up or got things wrong). I would ask my crew who was doing drag stag that night, I then stood that person down and I would do their shift instead. My men always wanted to know what I had done wrong, I would reply; "that is for me to know and for you to find out".

I think it became a bit of a mission for them to find out what I had done wrong. The main reason I enjoyed drag-stag was so that I could spend the night listening to the owls and nightjars depending on where we were in Germany. As dawn approached, I would sit in my trench or by a tree and immerse myself in the sound of the dawn chorus while everyone slept. During this time, I was of course hoping that we would not get bumped (attacked) by the enemy.

We had an unwritten rule that whoever was on drag-stag would wake the others with a brew. Back then my brew was coffee NATO Standard (NS), some of the guys preferred Warsaw Pact (WP). NS is white with two sugars and WP on the other hand, is black with no sugar. There are some other variations depending on which unit you are deployed with. There was one time in the early 80's when we got crashed out by SACEUR (Supreme Allied Commander Europe) and instead of deploying to our usual peacetime Active Edge location, we were deployed to a quarry, where we had never been before. I had been to this quarry on a regular basis to check on the resident Eagle Owls that bred there. The Eagle Owls were part of a very successful reintroduction programme to re-establish them back into Germany in all their glory. The Owls changed their location every two weeks, which meant that I had to relocate them.

I was taking a walk on a bright and very hot day on the prairie in Canada. I approached a lone leafless tree which was just off the beaten track at the 5-mile circle. As I got closer to the tree, I could see a nest on top of it. Suddenly, I felt a rush of air directly above my head, forcing me to duck. I looked up but could not see what it was as the sun was in my eyes. Several more times this happened, something was trying to attack me. As I withdrew, I got to see what it was, it was a beautiful Ferruginous Hawk, it was trying to protect its young. I managed to get it in my bins, and I could clearly see the rustic red of the legs against the all-white underparts as it soared overhead.

Prior to deploying for the 1st Gulf War in 1991 I was on another Med Man Exercise; part of our exercise included carrying out counter bombardment on ourselves. This was the first-time a British Artillery unit was to do this. It required three of the six guns in our battery to move to another location. Once in position, each gun section reported ready. It was then up to the OP's (Observation Post) to take it in turns to direct the fire power onto each position. The crews had to baton down inside their armoured vehicles. The aim of the exercise was for the men to experience the effects of a bombardment from an enemy force. While we waited for things to be set up, I of course took the opportunity to go birding. I managed to bag a Sprague's Pipit, as well as some great views of Chestnut-collared and McCown's Longspur. I even managed to locate two nests during this time, both of which had young in them. One of the things I really loved about the prairie was the sweet smell of the grass, it was strong and refreshing, and a joy to breathe in its distinctive smell. The order came to baton down and once they were in their vehicles and secure, the fire mission began.

I along with Phil and many others watched from a safe distance; I managed to take some photos of the shells exploding near to the guns. One of the shells landed inside the gun position, moments later a large piece of shrapnel landed within a few feet of where I was sitting. It was well over twelve inches in length by about six to seven inches at its widest point; what did I do? I picked up my helmet and put it on, as if that was going to make a difference. It would be like running a red-hot knife through soft butter. In hindsight I wondered what the hell we were thinking, we are not bullet proof. After the mission was over, I returned to the ammunition (ammo) compound; on the way we flushed a Hudsonian Godwit. It landed on the track we were on and then it flew a short distance and landed directly in front of us, forcing us to slow down. Each time we got close to it, it flew a short distance, and landed again, until it decided to fly off altogether it seemed to me that it was trying to lure us away, I suspect from its nest.

During one of the many briefings prior to being deployed to the Gulf we were told not to write home telling our family and friends where we were located; if anyone was discovered doing this they would be severely dealt with. I wanted my children to know where I was. The way I got around this problem was with the way I addressed my letters to them. I always addressed my letters with not just the date but also letters which indicated the place I was in for example: 4th January 1977 BNI = Belfast, Northern Ireland. For the Gulf War I came up with a similar plan. I decided to use the map from the 'Atlas of the Breeding Birds of Arabia' by Michael C Jennings. I dated my letters using the numbers and letters from around the edge of the map, for example: 1991 Jan **33 KA**.

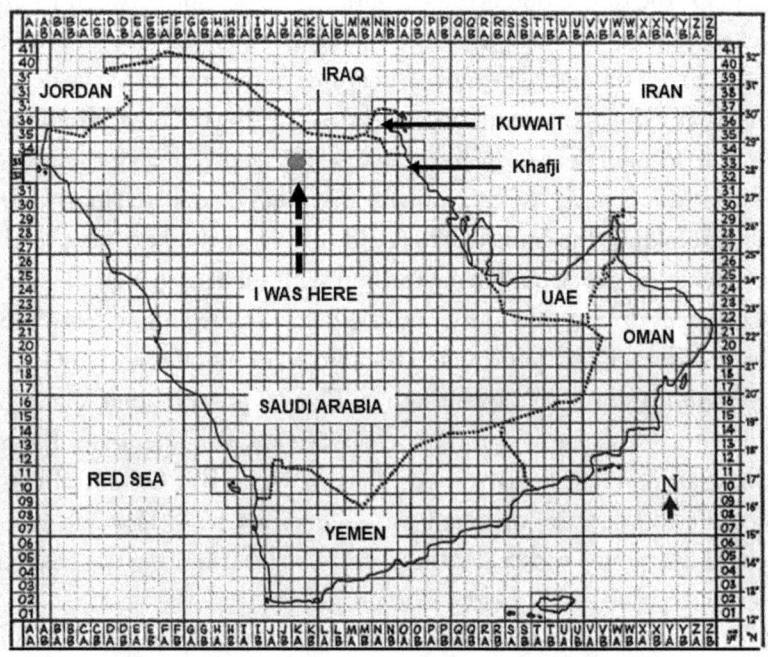

I pinned the map on my daughter's bedroom wall and showed them how to use it. All they had to do was find the relevant numbers and letters on the perimeter of the map, follow these two lines until they met up and that was where their Dad was. Strictly speaking, by the time they got my letters we would have been long gone from that location. Years later I met Michael Jennings at the British Bird Fair and I shared my story with him. He was excited by it and asked if he could use it in his next book, of course, I said yes. Before being deployed, Keith Pearce our BSM ordered all of the senior ranks into his office for a few final words. He ended the meeting by asking if there were any questions. I piped up, "it's not a question Sir, I just want say that every one of you F%$&ers will be birdwatching by the time the war is over, mark my words", I will let you guess what their response was. As we stood in the desert receiving our orders for the day, I watched as a Butterfly flew right between us and in close pursuit was a Dragonfly. I remember thinking that it seemed strange to see these two beautiful creatures in the middle of the desert. This was during the beat-up phase prior to crossing the breach into Iraq. We were located near to some pylon lines; I decided to go for a walk to see what was around, when I came across a large Arabian Spiny-tailed Lizard. Holding the muzzle of my rifle I placed the butt next to the lizard which it struck out hitting the butt with such force I felt the shock waves travel up my rifle to the muzzle break. It gave a few more good whacks, after which I left it alone. Richard was located elsewhere in the desert with his unit. We would write "Blueys" to each other about the birds we were seeing within our respective areas of operation. Blueys are blue airmail letters that are post-free known as BFPO 3000 (British Forces Post Office). In my area I was seeing Finsch's Wheatears, while Richard was seeing Hooded Wheatears. The bizarre thing was that our letters went via the UK, before reaching us.

I was awoken at 5am to the sound of what I can only describe as someone playing a flute, lying in my maggot (sleeping bag) I listened to this beautiful sound. This went on for several mornings and I began to wonder who could be playing a flute especially at five in the morning. I was not aware that any of my men could play an instrument let alone play it so well. I decided that I would find out who it was. At the end of my morning briefing I said to my men, "OK, which one of you is playing a flute at five in the morning?" They all looked at me as if I had well and truly lost it, "Boss what are you on about, has the prospect of the war got to you already?" came one reply, others believed I had just landed from Mars. I insisted one of them was playing a flute and it was OK as I thought it was wonderful. "Now we know you have lost it" came another response as they walked away laughing to get on with their tasks for the day. Calling after them I said, "okay, I will find out who it is", and so the next morning I awoke once again to this beautiful sound. Jumping out of my Scratcher (another term for sleeping bag), I started to head in the direction of the sound. I must have walked for about five minutes and after negotiating several sand dunes I eventually came to the place where the sound of the flute was emanating from.

I was drawn to look up and to my astonishment I saw a Greater Hoopoe Lark tumbling towards the ground; singing as it tumbled, falling like a stone towards the earth. I concluded that it was the lark's song bouncing off the sand dunes casting it all directions. At last I had found the source responsible for the flute like sound that greeted me in the morning. This has remained without doubt, one of the most beautiful bird songs I have ever heard. Such beauty in the midst of what we were about to enter into was something quite surreal. In amongst the horrors of conflict, beauty can be found.

One of my favourite places on earth, is not the jungle or the mountains although I do love these places, it's the desert. Throughout the first Gulf War (1991), opportunities for birding were surprisingly good. As we drove through the desert, I saw plenty of birds, mostly Waders and Sandgrouse but all were too far away to identify them properly. I would see birds in and around our cam-net (camouflage nets). I guess the birds were attracted to them because they looked like trees or bushes, and I suspect it was because they offered shade as well. The flies were certainly drawn to the nets, particularly if you dropped any food on the desert floor, this in turn provided the birds with a good supply of easy food, I guess you could have classed it as a Mc Flyby for the birds.

One day I found an injured Marsh Warbler hanging in my cam-net, (maybe it was not so good for birds after all). I rescued it, it appeared to have damaged its wing. I put it in a box and placed it in the cab of my truck. The next morning, I took it in my hands and presented it with the flies from around my cam-net, which it ate. Given that it was keen to eat, I was hoping that the damaged wing was not permanent and at some point, it would fly off. Sadly, it died a few days later, even though it was feeding well.

Returning to our location after an ammo run, I saw a Hoopoe sitting on top of my cam-net. On another occasion a Pallid (Hume's) Scops Owl was sitting on one of my cam-poles which supported my cam-net. As I arrived it flew a short distance from my vehicle and landed on the ground affording me some excellent views of it before flying off into the distance. One of my men opened the cab door to his truck and out flew an owl. Shortly after rainfall areas of the sand turned instantly into a lush blanket of green vegetation, soon after a lot of birds would appear; as we discovered from one of our road trips.

I remember arguing with Keith our BSM prior to moving into Kuwait, I wanted my guys to move with the guns, but the Americans said wheeled vehicles had to go a different route to the tracked vehicles. How weird is that; it just goes to show the pride you hold for your battery and the men in it, that you would stand in the middle of the desert in a war zone arguing the toss with your BSM about who goes which way. Somehow for me, it did not feel right to go into Kuwait without the guns.

We were now at the end of the 100-hour war and still based in the desert we had to do an ammo run into Saudi. Stan Harper asked if he could come with us as he needed to make a call home to sort out some details for his up and coming marriage, he even got baptised while in the desert. I always liked it when other members of the battery travelled with us. Our return trip back to Kuwait was not without its hazards. We drove through the city of Khafji. This is where the Iraqis engaged with the coalition forces in the Battle for Khafji, it was the first ground engagement. As we got closer to Kuwait, we encountered not just oil fires but many obstacles such as destroyed vehicles of all types in the road forcing our convoy to snake around them. It was around 14:00 hrs when we reached the oil fires and everywhere we looked there were fires with bellowing plumes of thick black oily smoke. The heat that the fires gave off was so intense that it replaced the normal heat of the day, we could feel it in our trucks, even with our windows closed. The fires were at least a mile or two away from the main road. Our windscreen was covered in oil, so we dare not put our wipers on and the sky was so dark from the oil that we had to put our headlights on.

Stan was driving Robo's truck at this point, it was Robo who came up with the idea of using the air filter cover on his truck as a wash bowl, in fact we came up with a few ideas to make life better for us. Dave Horrobin had the idea of putting MRE's (Meal, Ready-to-eat or field rations) inside the heater in the cab before a long move so that when we got to the next location, we had a hot meal and no water was used in the making of the meal. Another time, Scott Whitmarsh (my driver) and I drove past a pile of discarded ammunition boxes and sitting on top of them was a Red-breasted Flycatcher. I told Scott that I have to get back there and bag it as it would be a lifer for me. The desert really was full of life. Arriving back at the Gun Position, I commandeered Phil's JCB, much to his disgust. It is worth pointing out that I was the Fleet Manager for the Battery at the time and yes, I did use my rank to get my way, in my defence it was an opportunity not to be missed.

I was feeling very happy about getting this great little bird. I have not seen another Red-breasted flycatcher since. I gave Phil his JCB back, but this time he really was pissed with me. In the process of going for the flycatcher I managed to burn a hole in his Bergen from the exhaust pipe of his JCB. I felt my ears burning to the words of Merchant Banker (W%@ker). Sorry Phil.

After the war, it was decided that 127 Dragon Battery would remain in Kuwait in direct support of 3RRF (Royal Regiment of Fusiliers) who had lost nine men during what is commonly known a 'Friendly Fire'

attack. This is the discharge of a military weapon that injures or kills a member of one's own armed forces or an ally. Personally, I do not like this phrase; there is nothing friendly about a bullet chasing your arse, no matter what barrel it comes from. I prefer to call it 'Blue on Blue'.

The morale of my men took a major dive to ground zero as we watched convoy after convoy heading down the main highway towards Saudi Arabia, after all, they were all going home, and we were staying for another thirty plus days. Soon after, we had many visitors, General Schwarzkopf, being one of them and of course one of our own high-ranking officers whose name escapes me (apologies to the person concerned). He arrived with his shepherd's crook, sporting a Tam o' shanter on his head (a traditional Scottish bonnet). We were paraded in a half circle in front of him, he then proceeded to tell us all what a great job we had done and how our country was proud of us. Personally, I was very proud of my men without whom life would have been much harder. As he was delivering his speech, I caught sight of a Pallid Harrier quartering just above the ground, some distance behind the officer.

My focus switched to the Harrier and his words faded into the background that was until I became aware that a good number of the men were also watching the Harrier. As the bird passed out of view behind the officer, the bodies that were sitting on the desert floor leaned as one from left to right. I guess so that they could continue to observe the Harrier, and again right to left as the Harrier moved back the other way in its quest for food. I was stood behind the men with the other senior ranks and officers when I heard whispers moving down the line, one of the men in front of me leaned back and asked me "what kind of bird is it?".

To which I replied, "It's a Harrier". This information then moved back down the line like a concentric ring. Once again, I could hear the whispers moving back towards me like a wave, as the same soldier leant back again, he looked up at me and whispered, "isn't that a f@+%ing plane?!". I could hardly contain myself; I love Squaddie humour. In the moments when our thoughts were of home and loved ones, however well-intentioned, we had to listen to a speech. However the POWER of NATURE certainly played its role in keeping our SPIRITS up that day. Well, it kept mine up for sure. Later on, we joined up with 3RRF in a camp, the air was thick with oil and while eating a meal, droplets of oil rained onto my white plastic plate. That day I took a picture of the sun at ten in the morning, there was so much oil in the air that I could look directly at the sun.

Many years later I was chatting on the phone with Andy Tomkinson who was one of our officers at the time and now a good friend. He revealed that Dick Gardner (RIP) and Wally Walszak were on a wind-up mission with me. At the time they told me that they had seen a bird, and they wanted to know what it was so they proceeded to describe it to me. It was clear to me it should not have been there, in other words it would have been a rarity, I had to check it out; so off I went looking for it in the direction they had pointed me in.

At the time I had no reason to doubt them as I respected them (and still do), that said it was at this point I should have realised they were on a wind-up. Squaddies will always take any opportunity to take the piss. Their description of the bird was very convincing and of course it would be as they got it straight from my field guide without my knowledge, I do not actually remember now which bird it was. Nice one lads, but to find this out twenty-three years later, I ask you.

During the war, (I sound like grandad from Only Fools and Horses now) we were moving so fast, we didn't have time to pick up all our ammunition and load it back onto our trucks. Before moving into

Kuwait City, I had to send my guys back into Iraq to pick up the shells that we had dumped. On their return they told me about some of the things they saw, some of which I cannot put in this book. They said that they saw birds of prey picking up human body parts and flying off with them. This may sound distasteful but in nature nothing goes to waste and food in the desert can be hard to find. They may have also moved off of their migration route to 'exploit' a potential food source. We were eventually stationed in Kuwait City on an industrial estate which we named St Georges Lines. During our time there I needed to get my birding fix, but in order to leave camp, I needed someone to come with me. I asked around for volunteers and got none. In the end I had to go against my better judgement and order one of my men to come with me. I told him to bring a book because he would get bored, not being a birder. What made it worse for him was, after driving around for quite a while, checking out the local reedbeds where I only saw one duck and one shrike. We returned to camp and parked up outside the main gate where there was a small pond no more than few metres from the camp gate. Here, I ended up getting some great birds, the most notable being a Sooty Falcon that was flying low and fast parallel with the camp wall. It swooped over the pond at speed but failed to make a catch, the pond presented the Sooty with many birds to feast on as they dropped in for a drink; one of which was a striking Black-headed Wagtail which was working its way in and around the rocks looking for and catching insects.

Bosnia and Herzegovina (BH) also known as Bosnia, is a large region that has a moderate continental climate, with hot summers and cold, snowy winters. The southern tip of the country has a Mediterranean climate. My unit served there in 1996 as part of IFOR (Implementation Force), which was a NATO-led multinational peace enforcement force under a one-year mandate, and we were some of the first NATO troops to be deployed there. Bosnia is a beautiful country, especially if you are a birder. As I drove around the country visiting our various locations, I saw birds like the Eurasian Bittern resting in full view on an open plain, on the edge of a reedbed. There were also two Black Storks flying in the distance.

We were based in Jajce which was a beautiful town with an old castle sitting atop of a hill, and incidentally it was the best place to phone home from, the quality of the line was like being in the same room with my children. We were about 10kms from Šipovo where our hierarchy were based. The municipality covers an area of 510 km², much of which is forested, and from the road Tito's name could be seen on the forested mountainside where the trees had been felled to spell his name. My boss Iain Wilkie; nicknamed the Rottweiler or Rock for short is a short well-respected, proud Scotsman, while I was nicknamed Chihuahua. I never did find out why they called me that, compared to Iain, I am a tall proud Northern Irishman. One day Iain and I had an opportunity to take a different route from Šipovo, which meant going off road we skirted around a nearby lake, birding as we went. Along the way I bagged a Pygmy Cormorant for the first time. On another trip we came across some men dressed all in white at the side of the road, they were EU monitors investigating a mass grave found under a bridge. It had been blown up in a weak attempt to hide the bodies, and near to one of our gun battery's, a dead man had been found; his body surrounded by mines.

I guess they were hoping for someone to be killed trying to recover his body. Iain had to return to the UK. Nigel Helleyer (RIP), Iain's replacement arrived in theatre. It was agreed that I would show him around our area of operation to introduce him to key personnel and to familiarise him with the routes and locations of the Gun Battery's. We were issued with maps showing all the routes within our area of operation, and it just so happened that the route we took on this day was called Route Vulture. Nigel and I were chatting as we drove, when in the distance I could see a large white bird perched on top of a telegraph pole. As we got closer, I thought, that looks a lot like an Egyptian Vulture at which point Nigel's voice drifted into the background as I focused on this large bird. I thought to myself it can't be, surely, they do not come this far north.

As we got closer, I realised that it was indeed an Egyptian Vulture, so I slammed on the brakes, sharply coming to a halt as I jumped from the Landrover, Nigel leaped out at the same time cocking his weapon, effectively putting a bullet into the breach of his SLR (Self Loading Rifle). After which the conversation went like this:

Geoffrey:	"What are you doing?"
Nigel:	"Aren't we getting attacked?"
Geoffrey:	"No, don't be silly, I stopped so I could see the Egyptian Vulture on that telegraph pole" I was smiling and pointing in the direction of the bird.

At this point Nigel went right into one, shouting

Nigel:	"They F%@king told me about you! I wondered why they were laughing as I left the office!"

Once he had calmed down, he saw the funny side of it. I can only image what the guys told him before we left, perhaps it went something like this;

The Men:	"Where you off to then?"
Nigel:	"Geoff is taking me around to see the Battery's"

Big smiles and knowing looks cast in each other's direction.

The Men: "Good luck with your birding trip then, expect to be twitching all over the place"

Although I am sure the conversation was much, much more colourful than I have just described. The Egyptian Vulture was a lifer for me. After Route Vulture we went up onto Route Parrot towards the headquarters at Šipovo. We returned on Route Parrot, then went onto Route Cuckoo and up onto Route Pelican. Judging by the pattern of the names, I wondered if the originator of the routes was a Birder, as most routes were named after birds. The rest of the day was uneventful apart from when I saw a Great-spotted Woodpecker in camp, this bird appeared much redder and slightly darker than the Great-spotted seen in the UK or Germany.

One of the most profound moments I have had in my life was, not seeing dead bodies, not even blood and guts, it was something that seemed much simpler than that and yet it was exactly the opposite. The next day Nigel drove as we made our way back to camp; we were about half way when we passed a house which looked like something out of the Blitz. A woman was sitting on the grass verge, she was crying, and a man with his arm around her was trying to comfort her, perhaps he was her partner. There was another man nearby who looked like he might be the first man's brother. It took only a few seconds to pass them and the house; I began to wonder if this destruction in Bosnia could happen in the UK, in a way it had already happened with the conflict in

Northern Ireland but with fewer factions. I tried to visualise her daily life; getting up in the morning, packing her husband off to work with his lunchbox, giving the kids their breakfast and putting the washing out on the line before taking them to school. After dropping the kids off at school, maybe she went shopping. And now, it was all gone. All of it, not even a photo album to look back on the happy memories. I am often asked, what one moment changed things for me, and I am always transported back to that moment. I would go as far as to say that this was the beginning of my spiritual awakening, that I was aware of.

I went with Ken for a drive to have some downtime and of course do some birdwatching. We were on the other side of the Kupres Mountains when we came across the natural beauty of the Kupres Plateau. It's a little unknown part of the world, a place where an untouched landscape once existed. As we drove past some fencing, I braked and did an immediate U-turn telling Ken there was something different sitting on the fence we had just passed.

As we pulled up, sure enough there it was, my first encounter with a Long-legged Buzzard. This was a great find, because in my field guide it was a small dot on the map; occurring in a very small area separated from its main range. We watched this buzzard with its upright stance for a while before moving on. As we crossed back over the mountain, I glimpsed an Alpine Accentor dropping down from a wall as we drove past it. Reaching open land at the base of the mountain we saw Red-backed Shrikes singing from the top of every major bush along the side of the road. We decided to make a pit stop on our way back to Jajce; we found a nice spot to park off the road, it was a hot day and we sought the protection of the trees.

While sitting in the shade, I clocked movement in front of me. I really could not believe my eyes it was my first ever active Wryneck nest hole. The adults were toing and froing to the nest and their beaks were packed with food to feed to their young. While all around us was the glorious sound of Golden Orioles singing with their fluty, melodious song, they are a stunningly beautiful bird and masters of disappearance; it is difficult to see them against the tree canopy with the sun shining through the lush green and golden leaves. The adult male is unmistakable with its black lores on a golden yellow head. The broadly yellow-tipped coverts form a carpal patch on its black folded wings, which show as a yellow crescent in flight. The flight-feathers have narrow, pale yellowish tips and the tail is all black. The bill is a dark pink, its eyes are a deep maroon and its legs and feet are grey-blue. It is truly one of nature's beautiful birds.

When I returned from Bosnia, I went to see Peter Hoffmann a dear friend of mine. He along with two other families live in the same house in a village called Lipperode. Peter told me that when they got a letter from me after their evening meal, they would all sit together and Werner (RIP) would read out my letters. Peter said they always knew what state of mind I was in by my handwriting. You could say that they were the most unlikely people I would have as friends, that said, perhaps it was not so unlikely after all. They are the loveliest people you could wish to meet; the children are great, and I likened them and the house to the TV programme; The Little House on the Prairie, except I call their place; The Little House in Lipperode.

Approximately 1,000 kms (625 miles) east of the Falkland Islands, in the vast unforgiving Southern Atlantic Ocean, lays a small island scattered with ghost towns. At the turn of the 20th century these towns were established whaling stations, but decades later they were abandoned when whale stocks were depleted. They were killed off by the development of the factory ship which could process whales quicker and more efficiently at sea, leading to the decline in the whole industry. The island in question is South Georgia, it's extreme environment, with unobstructed storms sweeping in from the Antarctic, battering the island with raging cold winds, snow and driving rain makes it one of the most beautiful places on earth. As we walked around, the stations were deserted, the tables still laid with plates, cups and cutlery; the whaling towns are now museums, a reminder of a devastating phase of British history.

From end to end the island is about 95 miles, (150km) it's extremely mountainous with glaciers and fjords. South Georgia has been under British administration since 1908, except for a brief period in 1982 when Argentina occupied the island. It has never had a self-supporting or indigenous population and the famed explorer Ernest Shackleton stopped there in 1914 on route to his ill-fated attempt to cross Antarctica on foot. Today the main inhabitants are service personnel, penguins, seals and reindeer. The latter were introduced to the island by Norwegian whalers for sustenance and hunting. Vast chains, ramps and other mechanical mechanisms were used to haul the great whales up onto the shore and then onto platforms ready for dissection. Seeing this equipment and visualising what took place all them years ago personally affected me.

I had the opportunity to sail down to South Georgia on three occasions, but the first two trips had to be cancelled due to work commitments. I sailed down on the Grey Rover it was to be my first long voyage, a ten-day round trip with two days ashore. I felt somewhat apprehensive as I had not got any sea legs. The crew on the Grey Rover were a great bunch of guys. They had a good laugh at my expense as we left port, taking great pleasure in describing what my face looked like.

The journey there and back was very smooth and one of the crew told me that the sea is calm 75% of the time. The majority of my time was spent on deck, even though it was desperately freezing. Every now and then I would run inside and get myself a hot cup of sweet tea, I would then run back outside to the stern of the ship. The best time to be outside was just after a meal as the cooks would throw scraps of food overboard, and this of course drew in the birds. At times some of the birds were within three arm's length from me; birds like the Black-browed, Grey-headed, and Yellow-billed Albatrosses and a bit further out were the Wandering Albatrosses. I estimated one of them to be about a mile away from the ship and yet it was enormous, I can only describe it as the B-52 (Bomber) of the South Atlantic it was so big. At one point I thought I had spotted a Light-mantled Sooty Albatross just after we ran into a school of Pilot Whales which is a large dolphin. We sailed past Bird Island which often features in nature documentaries. This was a once in a life time opportunity; knowing that you're in a part of the world that very few people have had the privilege to be in. With the smell of the sea air, the freezing cold wind, and sea spray pounding every pore in your face, there was just something quite magical about it.

Just before dusk someone called out, they had caught a bird which had landed on the ship. I ran to see what was to be my first Wilson's Storm Petrel; I got to hold it before releasing it. It was essentially a small dark brown bird, except for a white rump and flanks. When in flight, its feet stick out beyond its square tail, the webbing between its toes is yellow, with black spots in pre-breeding individuals. With Bird Island now well and truly behind us, the ship drew as close to the shore as it could.

We anchored opposite one of the disused whaling stations and a small boat was deployed to pick up a Gurkha patrol that we were to transport back to Grytviken. Soon after we got underway, I was leaning on the railing's with sea spraying in my face as I watched a South Georgia Diving-petrel flying in a straight line at eye level, when it entered a wave that rose up in front of it, and coming out the other side on the same trajectory, I was amazed that such a small bird basically punched a hole through a large wave which appeared to have no effect on its flight path. I had got used to seeing King Penguins on land, now I was enjoying watching them porpoising alongside the ship this was a rare experience which inspired one of the drawings I did for the 'Breeding Atlas for the Birds of the Falkland Islands'. Cape and Snow Petrels were all around the ship as we anchored in Grytviken harbour. That night, I was up on deck and I could not believe my eyes, snow had settled on the surface of the sea, quite an amazing sight, it was like looking at a dried-up lake in Africa where large cracks of dry mud formed, now delete mud and insert snow, and that is what it looked like. The thick snow stayed on the surface for several hours.

I had difficulty sleeping that night due to the excitement of seeing icebergs of all difference sizes, one even flipped over in front of me, as it passed very close to the ship, and there was a massive iceberg located just outside the harbour in Grytviken. It was like a giant Lenor bottle, light blue in colour (other fabric softeners are available). Then there were the glaciers, throughout the night I heard several avalanches. One of my plans was to get some skiing in; I really wanted to ski in one of the most southerly remote locations on earth. Alas it was not meant to be, due to the avalanche's restrictions had been imposed on anyone wishing to ski.

The next day we went ashore, and I immediately went to work. My reason for being there was to set up a HF radio station so that the resident Gurkha unit could communicate with their folks back home. As you can imagine they were very isolated, there was no television or radio, only VHS videos and they only got them when the ship went down to resupply the island. With my work done for the day, I ventured out with a colleague from the Royal Military Police (RMP), I was on the lookout for the South Georgia Pipit which is the world's most southerly and the islands only songbird, as well as the only endemic bird. There is the South Georgia Shag which is a regional endemic. Until recently the major threat to the Pipits continued survival was from rats, this has since been put to bed with a major eradication programme. Walking along the shoreline, I spotted the Pipit feeding in and around the rocks and seaweed while the water kissed its feet now and then, it was a great find.

We were on our way to visit the grave of Ernest Shackleton to pay our respects to one of our greatest explorers; born on 15th February 1874 he died on the 5th January 1922. Shackleton an Anglo-Irish explorer was from County Kildare, Ireland. It was an extremely powerful moment to be stood before a man who had achieved such great things. I remember watching a documentary about his exploits where a group of modern-day explorers had attempted to reconstruct his journey. Shackleton had rowed from the Antarctic to South Georgia, assembled a rescue team and returned to save his crew. The modern-day explorers did not complete their journey, yet they had the luxury of modern equipment and clothing. This shows just how hardy people were back then, both men and women. It was a REAL honour to be in the presence of this great explorer's gravestone. Buried next to him was a sign of more recent times, and that was the grave of Petty Officer Felix Artuso (RIP), an Argentinian submariner from the 1982 Falkland's conflict.

We were heading back to Grytviken with our heads down and our hoods up, as we fought against the hard driving snow, it felt like our faces were being pebble dashed. Suddenly, we came face to face with a Weddell Seal resting on the shoreline. We stopped for a photo, it just looked at us, probably wondering what we were, it made no attempt to flee or attack. I was glad about that, as it was a big seal. We then moved on and paid a visit to the Neo-Gothic church which was pre-built in Norway and erected in Grytviken by whalers led by Carl Anton Larsen around 1912–1913 and consecrated on Christmas Day 1913. The church is arguably the most southerly church on earth, and it is where Sir Ernest Shackleton's funeral service took place. We then went on to visit the Museum and on arrival we met an interesting couple who were running the museum. They arrived on the island by yacht, I would hazard a guess that they were in their mid-50s. We got talking to them; they told us that they left Liverpool sixteen years previously having purchased their thirty-foot yacht. They had sailed pretty much around the world by the time we met them.

They were stopping over in South Georgia for a rest, to replenish and to raise funds for the next stage of their journey. They were a fascinating couple with plenty of stories to share, they had also done some work with the albatrosses on Bird Island. My colleague and I then walked back to Grytviken, we encountered many other birds and mammals along the way from Arctic and Antarctic Terns, Southern Fulmars, to Sea lions and Elephant Seals near to the glacier. I even found a tooth which had been split in half along its length; I believe it may have belonged to a Fur Seal judging by its size. All in all, an excellent day out and well worth the hardship. South Georgia was without doubt one of the most mind-blowing places I have ever been.

I was on leave from my unit having applied for and being granted an indulgence (discount) flight. I headed for Hong Kong before it was returned back to China. I wanted to visit the Mai Po Marshes which is a nature reserve located near Yuen Long. I had booked my accommodation at the research centre there; I arrived at the reserve, having paid the cab driver I turned around and I literally bumped into two German friends Andreas and Alfons. They were staying a short distance away on a housing estate and it was decided that I could pitch up with them for the duration of my stay. Mai Po holds many of the world's rarities, such as Black-faced Spoonbill, Red-headed Bunting, Olive-backed Pipit, and Styan's Grasshopper Warbler although the latter are hard to see, I got lucky and had two brief but good views of one. On one of our trips out we went up into the hills, Andreas discovered two adult Red-headed Tits with four young all sitting along a branch at eye level, this sighting turned out to be the first breeding record for Hong Kong. There were Chinese Egrets, a spring migrant and among the more common species were Curlews, Terek Sandpipers, Red-necked and Long-toed Stints, Greater and Lesser Sand Plovers as well as Red and Great Knot and the globally rare Asian Dowitcher. The rare Spoon-billed Sandpiper was present in good numbers as was another rarity the Nordmann's Greenshank.

The lagoons had Whiskered Terns, and I bagged a Pied Harrier cruising around, as I was watching it a local worker passed me by, he was smoking two roll ups at the same time. He had one in each corner of his mouth, curious. Mai Po is home to four species of Kingfisher namely Black-capped, White-breasted, Common and Pied. We took a boat trip out to one of the many islands there, on the way we bagged the vulnerable Aleutian Tern, we saw Black-naped and Great-crested Tern also. As we walked around the island, we had great views of a White-bellied Sea Eagle fishing; it was quite amazing to watch as it flew high over the still water, it banked left and slowly but surely descended; its legs extended in front of it, it smoothly picked up a fish from the surface of the water with no effort involved whatsoever.

I had to obtain a permit in order to gain access inside the perimeter fence that separated part of the marshes from Hong Kong; once we had passed the fence line we were effectively in China. Andreas and Alfons had already got their permits so they helped me to get mine. With the permit obtained, I was now allowed to enter the fenced off area to gain access to the hides at the end of a long wooden walkway. We had to be out by 18:00 hrs, otherwise the Gurkhas who patrolled that section of the border would lock us out.

One day, just as it was getting dusk, we were watching a Long-billed Dowitcher, as I checked my watch, I found that it had stopped so we decided to make our way back, only to discover the Gurkha's had locked the gate. I became worried as I was still serving in the army and now, I was locked out on the Chinese side of the border. Andreas said, "not to worry, follow me", we turned right and walked until the fence stopped dead, at which point we just walked around it. There was a tower a short distance away, however no one was manning it. I thought really, what was the point of locking the gates if you could just walk around the fence. That said I was feeling relieved that I was no longer at risk of causing a potential diplomatic incident.

We were near the mist nets at the ringing station, when good fortune shone down on us with a Black-headed Bunting caught in the nets; this was a great bird to end the trip with. Some months after our return from Hong Kong I met up with Andreas and Alfons. Alfonse's mum served us the most amazing Pumpkin soup I have ever tasted and as we ate and drank, we talked about the next trip we were planning. Independently of each other, it turned out that we had decided to go to Nepal on the same day and to the same location but in the end, I could not go as I was deployed to Bosnia.

There are many examples of extreme birding within the AOS, Chris Dickey, a member of 29 Commando R. A. he did a tour of Afghanistan, in which he was part of a six-man FST (Fire Support Team) holding the rank of Gunner (Private).

In 2008, he began a six-month deployment in Helmand Province, armed with a Minimi machine gun with a SUSAT weapon sight, 4,000 rounds of link ammunition, a lot of water bottles, digital camera, and a 'Birds of the Middle East' field guide. Having been briefed by some members of the AOS before departure, he embarked on what could be considered the most primitive and extreme form of birding; Chris called it birding 'on the hoof' around the FLET (Forward Line of Enemy Troops). Taking on a Taliban stronghold was Chris's first operation, they fought for ten straight hours in the blistering heat in confined, house to house fighting. Apart from firing his weapon in anger for the first time, being shot at and blown up by RPGs (rocket-propelled grenade launcher) and seeing his first dead Taliban. Chris explains what happened next. "I came across a new bird the Hoopoe; I spotted it flying to the ground from the tree, it came during a lull in the battle. Being shocked by the proximity of the bird (a few feet away), I let out a 'Oh my God', which unfortunately, everyone else mistook as meaning we were about to be out flanked on my side, thus causing a huge uproar!" Chris goes on to share other situations he encountered out there. "A memorable incident was when we were trying to find a sniper who had hidden his weapon under his shirt and was trying to escape. Whilst looking through my binos for the culprit, a bird flew across my field of view and landed. It was nothing but a blip on the desert floor, I was impressed that I found it, so I said 'aaha'. Unfortunately, everyone thought I'd found the shooter; they really were not impressed when I showed them the whereabouts of a Hobby instead".

Chris continues. "Once off the ground and back in Bastion where the coffee is strong, the showers are hot and the food is edible, I was able to go for morning runs again. During these periods of cool and general quiet (unless the US marines were scaring off everything with their squads jogging and chanting) I came across Blue-cheeked Bee Eaters, Crested Larks and a Verreaux's Eagle".

He explains that "using a SUSAT (Sight Unit Small Arms, Trilux) is a crude form of birding, my experiences of ornithology in Afghanistan have been immensely enjoyable with many memorable encounters, which have helped improve my identification and knowledge of birds in their habitats. I can safely state that Afghan birding is not for the faint-hearted and will probably be the most extreme form of birding that I will ever do". CAOS trip anyone?!

CHAPTER 7

The Zachariassee

I would listen for their distinctive calls echoing across the countryside as they approached the Zachariassee. Sometimes, I was not able to see them due to the weather being overcast, other times there they were in the clear blue sky, calling to each other as they flew past in their V-formations making their way south to their wintering grounds. I lived in hope that one day they would land at the Zach.

One day as I stood at the Zach, their calls were getting closer and closer. Then they came into view and I watched as they began to circle overhead, their long necks stretched, and their wings spread wide. I felt a real sense of excitement as they began to descend lower, and lower; my excitement grew each time they dropped lower in anticipation of them landing. They lowered their legs in preparation for landing; I could feel my excitement coursing through my body, it was a nice feeling. Then it exploded all through my body in a massive moment of excitement, as they alighted on the small island in the middle of our disused gravel pit; which had become an important nature reserve for our area.

I am referring to the Common Crane, at their peak they numbered one-hundred and twenty birds; they were the icing on the cake. The Zach had already made it as a nature reserve, with the support from the local farmers, villagers, and an unknown powerful supporter, and with birds like the Glossy Ibis, Goshawk, Golden and White-tailed Sea Eagle rocking up, it just got better and better. However, the cherry on the icing of a great cake was the Eurasian Bittern, we have an individual that takes up residence during the winter months. This bird had last bred in the surrounding area back in the late 1930's. No one believed me when I said that one day, we would get it back and there it was, in amongst the reeds, the same reedbed that became home to a singing Great Reed Warbler in the spring. On the opposite side of the lake and in amongst the reeds, there was a pair of breeding Marsh Harriers. All we needed now, was for the Bittern to breed.

In the early 80's I was a member of a local German conservation group called the ABU, Arbeit's Gemeinschaft für Biological Umweltschutz (translated; Association for Biological Environmental Protection). At that time there were twenty-one sites designated by the state as nature reserves and the Zachariassee was one of them. It was but a short distance from my camp and where I was living in Lippstadt in Nordrhein Westfalen, in Germany.

Each area was assessed for its potential as a nature reserve and I offered to survey the Zach, as I felt that this was a project, I could get my teeth into. My inspiration came from a gravel pit at Great Amwell in Hertfordshire, in the UK which had been turned into a nature reserve, resulting in it becoming a Site of Special Scientific Interest (SSSI). I was inspired by what they had done, and I felt I could do something similar with our gravel pit. The Zach is one of eight dredging lakes in the local area and so far, it is the only one designated as a nature reserve. Over the years I have encountered many amazing sights there, such as a Merlin in hot pursuit of a Cockatiel; it was inches from its tail, as the Cockatiel squawking wildly raced past me, a few feet over my head, shortly before reaching the road some 150 metres away, it fell silent.

I knew my patch intimately, 'patch' is a term for a place that birders visit on a regular basis. I visited the Zach three times a day for months; I also had a sit-spot where I would watch quietly, just being in the moment. At that time, it was perhaps more akin to alone time, as I was in the midst of some very personal difficulties. Once I watched deer swim across the lake and another time I was sitting in my car when I saw a Weasel with a Rabbit, it was dragging it down the road after having dispatched it. It paused for a while right next to my side of the car before carrying on dragging the rabbit which was weaselly three times its size (sorry).

On my visits, I monitored and recorded the birds that turned up, such as White-winged and Black Terns. Knowing the local birds well, put me in a good position to know straight away when something was out of place, like the Little Gull sitting next to a flock of Black-headed Gulls on the island. The second cherry on the cake, was the first breeding record of an Eurasian Oystercatcher for the county, it came from another gravel pit (Baggersee) in Niedersachsen, near to Nienburg where it was ringed. It bred on a raft I had put together in camp from a crate that housed the side-panel for a Stalwart also known as a Stolly, which is a highly mobile amphibious military vehicle. I used chicken wire to hold in a large quantity of bottles to help it float, it was then covered with small stones; which they breed on.

The raft was used by the first Cormorant that turned up at the Zach, sometime later we had a Cormorant arrive with an orange neck ring with the code C9 on it. It turned out that this Cormorant was ringed at Abberton Reservoir in the UK. The reservoir is located five miles south-west of Colchester near the village of Layer de la Haye. Abberton was one of my regular patches when I was stationed in Colchester. How random is it that? I found it fascinating that when a bird of prey turned up, the male Oystercatcher would chase them away, because it had a sitting female and young to protect. However, when an Osprey turned up it was the only one the Oystercatcher would pursue beyond the fence for up to ½ km or more. All the other birds of prey he only chased them as far as the first fence. I am still trying to work out why.

Over the years, more than two hundred and fourteen species of birds have been seen at the Zach. Some of the birds that have been reported range from Red-throated, Great Northern and Black-throated Divers, Great-crested, Red-necked, Slavonian, Black-necked and Little Grebes, and then there are the waders of which there was no shortage. Peter once saw a Kestrel sitting on a fencepost, he observed it systematically drop down, and take the young of a pair of Ringed Plovers, returning to its post each time. Within a few hours they had all been eaten.

As part of getting the Zach recognised as a Nature Reserve, we needed to draw up a habitat plan, which I took on. We had a meeting at the Zach with an official from the County Government (Kreisverwaltung). Prior to the meeting Peter and I went over the plan, I said to Peter that I had put six hides on the plan and Peter said that we would never get six hides approved, I asked him to go along with me. We gave our presentation during which I asked the official for six hides, at which point he did what we call in the Army, the 'Echelon Puff', in Civvie street it is also common. By this I mean the person rubs their chin/neck, exhaling long and slowly, followed by the words, "oohh, I don't know, it could be expensive, it's a difficult job". I asked the official what he could give us. He responded with "I can let you have one", smiling, I said that we will take it. I smiled because one hide is what I had wanted, if I had asked for one, we wouldn't have got any, that's for sure. Of course, we would have loved more but they would come with time. In order to reduce the cost of the work we needed to do; such as put in ponds, channels and other labour-intensive work. I had managed to secure help from the Royal Engineers, after a site visit, they were well up for it. It was an all-round winner, the State saved money, it was great for Public Relations (PR) for the British Army, and we got what we wanted over a ten-day period. Sadly, it never happened. In the end we had a single bulldozer come out to the island, it did less than one percent of the work and was left there for about six weeks doing nothing.

Now that we had permission to build our hide, we needed funds for the materials. I entered into a competition in which our project got first place for our region. The judges had all said that we should have won the overall 1st prize for BAOR, but because we were outside of the BAOR network, they had to change the rules slightly to allow us to take part; therefore, we could not really win the first prize. But still, happy days, we won 700 D-Mark. The hide was built in camp with the expert guidance and help from Mick Lloyd, without whom it probably would not have been built. It seems people were taking bets on whether we would get the hide out of my garages or not, which of course we did, but only just. Having laid the foundation on site it was now time to move the hide to the Zach, with help from Tim our Recovery Mechanic, he lifted, and dropped it into place at the reserve using the crane on his recovery vehicle. We now had the only hide for the county.

As part of our conservation day the lads from 127 (Dragon) Battery, helped to dig ponds; build and launch another raft on the opposite side of the island. At our request, Graham our BSM, donned his diving gear and searched the lake to see if any old cars or oil drums had been dumped into the water, what happened next, we were not excepting.

Graham surfaced waving to me he shouted, "You have F%@king Jellyfish in here". I looked at Peter, told him what Graham had said, we then went out in our boat to investigate. We took some water samples, and sure enough there they were freshwater jellyfish, which were approximately one inch in diameter. What a great surprise that was, we presumed that they got there in the feathers of ducks, grebes and other water birds flying in from around the country, and no doubt the mussels along the banks arrived the same way.

One of the local policemen, who kept a rare breed of Scottish cattle, asked if he could graze them on the reserve, and of course we said "yes". The officer and his colleagues would from time to time patrol the Zach, which felt good to us while they were checking on his cattle, indirectly the Zach was looked after as well by the GCP (German Civil Police). Having discovered that someone had dumped paints and other chemicals in a bag at the Zach, Peter called the GCP. On inspection of the contents they found an address, the guy in question was given a large bill for the removal and disposal of the bags and their contents and I believe he also received a fine on top of that.

We also used the unemployed, known as the 'Ini' they would arrive with a supervisor and we would set them to work. At the end of the day we would sign their papers to say they had worked for us and had done a good job; they could then draw their unemployment benefits. What a great system. On one occasion the supervisor tried to show them how not to let a fire get out of control. However, his fire got out of control, the man was then in fear of his job and expecting a fine from the German Fire Service. Luckily, it was kept quiet and he got away with it, the bonus for us was that two species of Heather started to grow. Peter researched it and found that over a hundred years ago the area was covered in heather.

Many people would gain access to the reserve to sunbathe because it was so quiet and devoid of people. I recall a time when Peter and I were at the Zach, we saw a car driving away from us having thrown a pizza box out of their car window. Unfortunately for them they had to come back our way as there was no other way out. Peter waved them down and when they stopped, he threw their pizza box back at them through the car window and he gave them short thrift.

I was amazed by this, and I enjoyed it as well, why you wonder? Peter is one of the most relaxed people I know, so to see him enraged was not the norm. I watched the kids as they drove away with a flea in their ear and the look on their faces was awesome to see, they were not very happy teddy bears.

I recall onetime when I was watching a White Stork eating an eel it had just caught, I spotted someone on the Island. I rushed over to find out what they were doing. The person I met there was the bulldozer driver, we had met and chatted previously, back then he asked me why he had been asked to work there, and literally in that moment, a few feet away, two Broad-billed Sandpipers walked past us. I pointed at them and said you are here for them; you're providing them a place to rest over and to fatten up before they continued on their migration. The other people with him approached us and he introduced them as his wife and children, he said he wanted to share with them the work he was doing for nature protection.

I thought about how great it was that the Zach had made an impact on him and no doubt his children. He looked so proud that day. Peter managed to set up a stall in town with the local hunting lobby, to the best of our knowledge this had never been done before. The following year people thought we had a falling out with them because we did not repeat it, this was not the case. The only group that would not come on board with us was the local angling club. Sometime later I told Peter that we had someone fishing the reserve, and that they were being very careful not to leave any rubbish, line or hooks behind, in fact the only sign I found was where this person had been sitting, so we decided to try and catch whoever it was. That is, until Peter attended a party, he was approached by someone who said to him, "are you aware that you have someone fishing at your lake?", Peter replied "yes, we are trying to catch the person", the response back was, "word to the wise, don't".

Over time, we not only got unsolicited funding from the State, but we were given access to a set of documents and asked to ringfence the areas we would like as potential reserves for the future. It seems two men turned up at Peters house handed a large folder over and said we will be back in a few hours to collect it. Peter asked who they were, to which they said, "more than our job is worth to tell you, friend" and promptly left. Peter called me and said, "get over to my place now", and when I arrived, he shoved this very large file in front of me. The best way to describe it is as follows: when the local authorities are planning improvements, they draw up plans and put them out to consultation to all the parties that it will affect. This could be from building a new road, or new houses to an industrial estate and so on. We were given access to official and confidential documents by an employee of the Conservation Agency, which he provided to us without permission so that we could plan better. Meanwhile the birds kept rocking up at the Zach, with breeding Icterine Warbler, Peregrine Falcon, Water Rail, and Golden Oriole, some of the non-breeding birds were Avocet, Grey, Sociable and Golden Plovers, Turnstone, Woodcock, Stone Curlew, as well as Penduline Tit, Ringed Ouzel and Red-backed Shrike, just to name a few.

Peter and I had talked about having a meeting with the locals, we wanted to let them know what we were doing in the hope of getting them on board with us. We decided to have a BBQ at the Zach as opposed to an indoor meeting around a table where people would be guarded. A BBQ is informal; it was felt that people would talk more freely, politicians were not invited although they would turn up anyway, because they had not been invited. Sadly, I could not be there as I had an appointment with the First Gulf War. While I was in the desert Peter wrote to me to tell me how the meeting went. It was a resounding success with his skilful diplomacy Peter got everyone on board, especially the famers who agreed to move a road further down from where it was, at their expense. In fact, the meeting went so well, farmers from outlying areas wanted us to work with them, the politicians did turn up, uninvited.

As our relationship with the locals grew, the Zach went from strength to strength. There was one time we wanted to buy a field from one of the farmers, because there was a rare bird for our area breeding there.

However, the farmer did not want to sell his field, even though we could have enforced the law and made him sell it. We asked him why he wouldn't sell, he replied, "my grandfather and, my father were farmers, it's all I know, if you take this from me where will it end and what will I do?". To put this into context, this farmer went on his first holiday ever around that time, he phoned the farm every day to see how his cows were doing; in the end it was too much for him, and he came back early to be with his animals. On that basis we could not force him to sell his land, so we dropped the matter. Other interesting finds at the Zach were the bones of Woolly Mammoth, Woolly Rhinoceros and Giant Elk, plant wise we had a carnivorous plant called Drosera, commonly known as the Sundew.

In the meantime, many of the surrounding areas were purchased by a Nature Conservation Foundation (NRW Foundation for Homeland and Nature). The foundation provided us with one million Deutsche Marks. It took 10 years for the money to be used up and 11ha of new land to be added. Today the Zach is 145ha in size, when we started the project, it was only 33 ha.

CHAPTER 8

The Americas

I was waiting on the runway at Port Stanley, in the Falkland's, reflecting back on what a great time I had there, not just birding but all round and thinking about the RAF Sgt who tried to stop me from going to South America. Uninvited, he quoted some rule in a book that said I could not go to South America directly from the Falkland's. I told him to leave my office and come back with the rule book, then and only then, would I consider his request, if you can call it that, I am of course giving you the very polite version of what happened.

My flight was delayed due to the fact that Argentina would not allow the Lan Chile twin propelled aircraft to fly through their airspace. After several hours of waiting we were allowed to fly, I was told that this had become normal practise. The flight took seventy-five minutes, we flew quite low and because of this I was able to see whales breezing along the ocean. I could not tell which whales they were, I just bathed in the joy of seeing them from above. My flight was to Santiago, stopping over in Punta Arenas for a few hours, sadly I did not get a chance to bird outside the area, otherwise Magellanic Plover would have been my target bird.

I had been communicating with an RAF Sgt at the British Embassy in Santiago and he arranged accommodation for me. One of the civil servants agreed to put me up and I stayed for a few days at her apartment before heading onto Paraguay. I went out for a meal and a few drinks with the RAF Sgt and other embassy staff. I really enjoyed the Chilean night life, there was lots of great seafood, dancing and many, many pisco sours, a South American classic drink of both Peru and Chile. My host and I were chatting about how things were in Chile when it emerged that there was an air show about to start; at the same time Lady Thatcher was visiting, and part of her visit included the air show. Allegedly; it seems that the British Ambassador was worried about her visit. The Chilean Airforce had been given a Harrier Jump Jet as a kind of thank you for their support during the Falklands War. The Chilean Airforce had been told by the Ambassador not to put the plane on display as they did not want to upset the Argentinians. I was curious as to how it would turn out, the show was on while I was out of the country, so I had to wait until my return to find out the outcome.

Paraguay turned out to be an interesting country in many respects, I was once told by a South American that not even South Americans visit Paraguay, perhaps that's why I like it so much, apart from the birds of course. I had planned to meet up with a guy who was to be my birding guide. On arrival, I was picked up from the airport and after checking in to my hotel I was directed to a local travel agent. It turned out that my guide had cancelled our field trip, he had left it for the travel agent to inform me. With the help of the travel agent it was up to me now, to sort out the places I wanted to visit.

I decided to travel to the Tri-Border area between Paraguay, Argentina and Brazil. I wanted to visit Foz do Iguaçu one of the largest and most stunning of the world's waterfalls running off from the Iguazu River which is located between the borders of the Argentine province of Misiones and the Brazilian state of Paraná and forms the boundary between Argentina and Brazil. Together they make up the largest and, in my view, the most stunning waterfall system in the world, the falls divide the river creating an upper and lower part of the Iguazu River. The first European to discover the existence of the falls was a Spanish Conquistador called Álvar Núñez Cabeza de Vaca back in 1541. I wanted to see the Blond-crested woodpecker, with every movement this bird flicks its crest, because of this it is known locally as the Marilyn Monroe of the woodpecker world.

The falls are home to the Great Dusky Swift, hundreds of them can be seen flying through the mist of the water as it plummets towards the lower river, as they head for their nests, located on the rocks behind the waterfall. I stayed in a very cheap hotel costing $2 a night. However, I left the next day as I did not feel safe, so much so, I propped a chair against the door handle and placed my Bergen on the chair to act as a makeshift alarm system. The room had its own eco-system with a Praying Mantis lurking on top of the shower head, which I did not mind so much, and what I thought was a waterbed turned out not to be, it was the movement of bugs under the mattress that threw me, overall the place appeared very seedy. The next morning, I jumped on the bus and headed back into Paraguay arriving at the city of Ciudad del Este which featured in the 2006 film Miami Vice. I had not passed through any border control, I thought it might be located at the main bus station, but this was not so. As I waited for my bus back to Asunción, an American military truck drove past with troops in the back. I asked a local if he knew why they were in Paraguay, he answered by saying that they were drug running (allegedly); I am not so sure I believed him. Given that Ciudad del Este is a city of all sorts of goings on, I guess anything is possible?

I got the next bus to Asunción and back in my hotel I pulled out my travel guide, which I had been given but had not read. If I had read it, I would have known to get the bus driver to stop on the bridge at the border, where upon, I had to ask him to wait while I made my way down the embankment and under the bridge to get my passport stamped at the border control which was located there. I had entered Paraguay illegally. I had an exit stamp from Paraguay and entry stamp into Brazil, but no exit from Brazil or entry into Paraguay. I wondered why a passport control point would be under a bridge, which was on the main artery into Paraguay? I can only conclude, if you don't see it you don't need to stop it or search it. However, I do know that the US often run joint exercises in that region, mostly in the Paraguayan Chaco.

The bus I was on was for locals who are not required to have their passports checked all the time, if indeed they have one.

The Gran Chaco is sparsely populated, a hot and semi-arid lowland region of the Río de la Plata basin. It is divided between Eastern Bolivia, Western Paraguay, Northern Argentina and a portion of the Brazilian states of Mato Grosso and Mato Grosso do Sul, where it is connected with the Pantanal Region. The Argentine Chaco is great for birding, while there I was shown the nest of a Black-bodied Woodpecker crossed with a Lineated Woodpecker. At the Argentine and Paraguayan border crossing I came across two signs; the first one read: 'the Malvinas

(Falklands) belongs to Argentina' and the second sign read 'The only thing better than an Argentinian is another Argentinian'. My first trip to Paruaguy I travelled by bus to the Paraguayan Chaco. It was late when I got off the bus from Asunción at Cruce Los Pioneros, I literally stepped into a one-horse town; consisting of a motel, a garage, and a restaurant with a small shop. The reception of the motel was dimly lit by a light from behind the desk. I threw my Bergen to the floor so I could check in, and that action was greeted by a roar; I turned to discover that my Bergen had landed on the motels pet Puma, who was none too pleased by what I had done. I on the other hand, was very pleased that it was not that pissed with me. The next day, with the help of a local guide, I drove around the area and bagged a Cream-backed Woodpecker; a handsome bird indeed. There was also a Checkered Woodpecker near to the motel. The Chaco has many water birds, and it's a good place to pick up migrants like the Mississippi Kite and on route there are many good places to stop for birding. Jabiru Stork, Nanday Parakeet, and Plumbeous Ibis are just a few of the birds I saw from the main highway. I bumped into a Greater Rhea which is a pretty cool bird to come across in the bush; other birds of interest in the Chaco were the Coscoroba Swan and the White-headed Marsh Tyrant; this little bird really made an impression on me. The male is all black, apart from its relatively large white head and yellowish lower mandible. The female has brown wings and upperparts and a black tail. The sides of her head and forecrown are dull white. It is a quiet bird and is found in marshy savannahs and reedbeds. I enjoyed watching them pick off insects from the vegetation on the surface of a pond, they also sit on low exposed perches in the marsh vegetation, or on a branch, occasionally sallying out to feed on passing insects, before returning to the same perch just like a flycatcher.

Pedro Juan Caballero is on the western border with Brazil. I had planned to meet up with the ranger from the National Reserve there; I had a note written for me in Spanish by my very helpful travel agent;

it explained what I wanted to do. I gave the note to the bus driver, he looked shocked and said to me, "no señor bandidos, bandidos", he was telling me the place was dangerous and full off bandits. I thought I would go anyway and assess the situation when I got there. After a few hours the driver refused to stop for anyone, including school children trying to hitch a ride.

This was now looking serious, and I became aware that people were taking an interest in me and wondering if I would get off the bus or not. One guy showed a keen interest in what I was doing, he was expressing offers of help, I was now becoming uncomfortable. The bus stopped and I got off, the plan was to walk 1.5 kilometres into the bush and spend the night in a hut. However, my timing was out as I had hoped to get there in daylight hours and meet the ranger the following morning. I looked around, the place was in the middle of nowhere and it was pitch black. I decided not to even sleep by the side of the road let alone walk into the bush at night, so I opted to get back on the bus, therefore no birds were seen on that trip. One of my travel rules is to always listen to the locals, even if I dip out on birds. Over the years I have heard some horror stories about people who did not listen to local advice. I was once stopped in Hong Kong by a local; he asked me where I was going. I said that I wanted to head up to the hills behind the houses of the area I was in. He said, "It's best not, even the dogs carry machetes here", I thanked him and made an about-turn and headed back.

In Pedro Juan Caballero I got the bus back to Asuncion, the chap who was chatting to me on the bus offered to help me find a hotel. He also said that he was a friend of the ranger, and he would take me to him in the morning. I was very wary of him at this point, I was thinking that this may be some kind of come-on and I could be walking into a trap of some kind. I insisted that I was going to get the bus back that night. He showed me where to get the bus and left, only to return later to check that I was okay. I thanked him for his help and offered him some money, but he flatly refused it. I felt like I had insulted him because he turned

out to be a really decent bloke. I guess if I had trusted him, I would have bagged loads of new birds. However, it is better to be safe than sorry.

Over the years I returned to Paraguay many times while still serving in the army. On one particular trip for some odd reason I decided to put British Soldier as my occupation on the green card. I have no idea why I did that, normally I would just write truck driver. Later, I had been told by someone in my hotel that there were rumours of a possible military coup, I saw some military activity in the form of aircraft flying around the capital, although I have to say they were so old that if you bombed them up they would not get off the runway.

The next morning, I went into the capital to pick up some provisions. Immediately after getting out of the car that I hitched a ride in, another car pulled up alongside me, a man got out, the car then drove away, and the man waited for me to pass him he then proceeded to follow me. At first, I thought that I was imagining things, however after fifteen minutes he was still behind me, so I decided to stop by a railing at the corner of the road and have a cigarette. He walked past me, crossed the road, and then stopped by the railings on the other side of the road. I could see him looking at me from his reflection in the shop window. I decided to duck into a store and leave by another entrance. As I stood by the other exit another person came around the corner and on seeing me, she became startled. Maybe it was my imagination, but she seemed to have a look of recognition on her face. I decided not to hang around and I left the city and headed back to my hotel; I thought, if I am not being paranoid, then I need to come up with a plan should a coup really happen.

Sitting on my bed I began to come up with an escape and evasion plan, given that I had put soldier on my green card I was not prepared to take any more risks in a country that had for years been run by a dictatorship. I had two plans; the first was to head for the British Embassy and failing that, I would head for Bolivia via the salt lakes in Argentina. In the end nothing happened. Maybe it was just someone in power posturing, still, I remained alert just in case. If it had turned out to be a coup, and I had managed to get out of the country, I thought I would write a book and call it Bravo Four Zero, I'd have maybe made a bob or two on the title alone?

I now had to get out of Paraguay and into Chile, the travel agent sent me to one of their contacts; this really was a case of who you know and not what you know. When I got there, I had to explain how I got into the country. Thankfully I had kept my bus ticket which I handed over to the official as proof of entry. The lady wrote me a note; she then phoned someone at the airport. After the call she said that at the airport I had to present myself and the note to Señor Caballero who would take care of things. Señor Caballero spotted me in the line for checking in, he came over to me and I handed him the note. He asked me to follow him, which I did. He led me through a side door and into immigration where my bags were searched by two women who looked like they could have been part of an occupation army in some old war movie. One asked me what my telescope was and as I explained it, it became clear that they had never seen one before. I offered to set it up for them so that they could have a look through it; they took it in turns to look at the aircraft on the runway; they seemed impressed by it. They then cleared me to take my flight to Chile. It would be fair to say that on this particular trip birding took a bit of a backseat; and it did not end there. As I arrived in Chile, I became worried as the Chileans tend to be more thorough with their passport checks. As it happened, luck was on my side, the guy checking the passports seemed to be a sprog (a military recruit or trainee). He did something wrong when checking the passport of the guy in front of me and his mentor who was stood behind him started to tell him what he should have done, at the same time the young man stamped my passport without checking it thoroughly. Had he done so he would have seen that according to my passport I was missing for four days. I grabbed my passport and made it on my toes out of the airport.

Outside the airport I negotiated with a taxi driver to get me back to the embassy apartment; it was agreed that I'd pay ten dollars US. On arrival, I paid the driver and as I went to get out, I found that the door was locked. He refused to open it unless I paid him another ten dollars (brave fellow I have to say). I reminded him that we had agreed a price and he should now open the door, but he refused. Rather than grabbing him by his throat I instead got my sleeping bag out of my backpack, he asked me what I was doing, to which I replied, "we agreed ten, if you are not going to let me out, I am going to sleep". He tried saying that I was a rich westerner and I could afford it. I laughed, and said "a deal is a deal, go about your business I will get my head down". He eventually saw sense and opened the door. As I left, he shouted "you drive a hard bargain".

The next morning, I was having breakfast with my host in her apartment when I asked her how the air show went. She began to tell me all that had happened. I will share this with you now, although I give no guarantee to its accuracy; all I can tell you is what I was told. Allegedly. The Argentines who were attending the air show, arrived with the words Malvinas belongs to Argentina painted on their aircraft fuselages. The ambassador was concerned that if Lady Thatcher saw the Harrier this could cause problems and he would have to clean up the mess afterwards. The day came, the press were there, the Chilean Airforce Commander presented himself to Mrs Thatcher and invited her to inspect his honour guard. After the inspection, he said that he had something to show her, and led her towards a hanger.

The ambassador, realising what was about to happen, approached her and said that under no circumstances was she to say a word; apparently, she nodded. The hanger doors rolled back revealing the Harrier. Lady Thatcher walked up to it, with her handbag over her arm, she turned to face the cameras and without saying a word, she stroked and patted the nose cone of the jet and smiled. Cameras flashed all over the place and the Argentines spat their dummy out and left. Without saying a word, Lady Thatcher allegedly made her mark by managing to cause a diplomatic incident. On my return I was expecting to see it all over the papers and politicians on the news trying to dumb it down. Instead, there was nothing, other than a small headline; 'Mrs Margaret Thatcher had to return from her trip to Chile early due to heat exhaustion'. She had indeed, suffered from a heat stroke and had collapsed while delivering a speech.

During my time in Belize I encountered my first Trogon. I could hear its soft call in the distance, I attempted to mimic its call, in order to discover what species of bird it was. Sure enough it worked and I watched as a beautiful Violaceous Trogon flew towards me on its short but strong wings; and landed not too far from where I was.

This bird has been in existence for more than forty-nine million years and in that time, it has developed the skill for staying close to the observer but remaining difficult to see; it seems that they like to remain hidden. Once located it is often their distinctive tail patterns that help to identify which Trogon I am looking at, even if I cannot see all of their bright colours. All the Trogons I have seen to date have had a distinctive tail pattern making it easy to identify them.

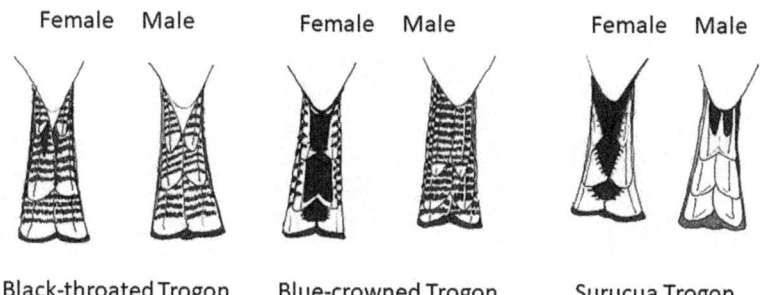

Black-throated Trogon   Blue-crowned Trogon   Surucua Trogon

Trogons are cavity nesters, which they dig out of rotting wood or termite nests, although one species, the Violaceous Trogon, prefers wasp nests. Incidentally, the name, Trogon, means to gnaw, although the Cuban Trogon seems to favour using woodpecker holes and shows less interest in gnawing out its own nest hole. In order to do this the wood needs to be strong enough not to collapse but soft enough to dig out a cavity, maybe the trees in Cuba do not fit the bill (no pun intended). Trogons have been observed landing on dead tree trunks and slapping the wood with their tails, presumably to test the firmness of the wood. They are generally inactive outside of infrequent feeding flights.

Their lack of activity is possibly a defence strategy against predation. They seem to like keeping their less brightly coloured backs facing the observer, while their heads, like owls, can turn slowly through 180 degrees enabling them to keep watch on the watcher. Their short legs and feet are weak, Trogons appear to be unable to walk beyond an occasional shuffle along a branch. They are even incapable of turning around on a branch without using their wings. It seems Trogons may have broken away from Africa, in much the same way as humans did. While the New World holds the majority of Trogon species, fossil records go back forty-nine million years to Germany, and even older in Denmark.

Shortly after leaving the Army I went off to Belize for five months working for Raleigh International as their Logistics Manager, it was the best thing that could have happened to me at that moment in time. I had been sacked from two jobs in Aldershot and shortly after that I turned down a guaranteed job; offered to me by one of my former Sergeant Majors, who had said I could do the job with my eyes shut. It was during the five-month period in Belize that I realised I wanted to work with people rather than do some routine job that I could actually do with my eyes shut. I loved working for Raleigh; I had many experiences while I was there. We lived in the former Guatemalan embassy six and half miles from Belize City. Just across the road from our headquarters was a large river, where I would often see Manatee's and Crocodiles swimming past as well as dolphins. I got out as often as I could to the project sites for which I was responsible, from Corozal in the north down to Punta Gorda in the south and from El Pillar in the west on the Guatemalan border, over to the two off shore islands Cary Cay and Coco Plum in the east. I never got to go to Belize with the army, so no patrolling and no bullets along the Guat (Guatemala) border. I tried once but was told I could not go because my Battery Commander at the time said I was only going for the birdwatching. The guy they were sending did not want to go and had no experience of working in an FDC, where as I did want to go and had experience of working on FDC's, of course, the added bonus was birding.

It was during a very long off-road drive to our jungle site in the west that we met with what appeared to be a Special Forces (SF) mobile patrol; we spent some time chatting with them before heading off to our location. We stayed in a large wooden lodge which looked out over a tree covered valley, some trees stood taller than others, which made them good for finding large distant birds. In the branches that afforded shade, there were Toucans with their beaks open, resting and seemly enjoying the cool breeze. A squadron of squawking Parrots would race by every now and then. High in the sky there was the silhouette of a large bird of prey riding the thermals and of course many other unidentified LBJ's (little brown jobs) going about their daily routines. The Parrots did a good job of being my alarm clock; one morning I also woke to the sound of a woodpecker calling. Leaping from my bed I followed the sound, which was coming from behind our lodge, I did not see the woodpecker, because I encountered a magnificent looking Ocellated Turkey instead. There is an expression, 'see the beauty in ugly', well I have to say that the Ocellated really fits that bill, for a turkey. It is possible I mistook the start of the male turkeys call for a woodpecker. The Ocellated is the smaller of the world's two species of turkey. Endemic to the Yucatan Peninsula reaching into Belize and Guatemala and despite a recent decline in the population they seemed to have bounced back from the brink of extinction. Both sexes have a fleshy blue crown which is adorned with nodules that vary in colour from red, orange, and yellow the male's nodules being more pronounced. They have a distinct eye-ring of bright red-coloured skin, especially visible on adult males during the breeding season. The tail feathers in both sexes are bluish-grey and each with a well-defined, blue-bronze eye-shaped spot, followed by a bright golden tip. Its upper wing bars are a rich copper and highly iridescent. Males also have spurs on the back of their legs.

I was heading to Corozal our most northerly site and on route I stopped for a bite to eat. In the café two of the meals on the menu stood out; one was Rice and Beans, and the other was Beans and Rice, both were priced the same. I asked the lady who was serving what the difference between the two was, she replied "Rice and Beans is where the beans are placed on top of the rice, and Beans and Rice is where they are both mixed up together." I said to her, perhaps she should charge a few cents more for mixing them up, after all it did involve a little bit of extra work, she laughed. As well as checking on the various project sites around the country, my task in this case was to check on the staff and volunteers as there were a few issues that needed resolving. I was also there to carry out a search for the American Flamingo which were suspected of breeding in the mangroves. As I drove through the countryside to get to the project site, I saw some Mennonites tending to their fields; they were all dressed uniformly, just like in the TV programme The Walton's. Having dealt with the issues on site, it was decided that we would head out the next morning to look for the Flamingo's.

We were woken up by the dawn chorus of the local Plain Chachalaca's clucking very loudly, they looked like a kind of turkey. After breakfast we set off in our canoes and headed for an area that the locals never ventured into. The water was very clear, the day was lovely and warm, and along the way I could see lots of small bird's like Yellow Warblers flitting in and out of the mangroves. At one point I jumped into the water to cool off, the bottom looked firm, however, on entering the water I sank up to my knees before making solid ground. Thank God it had not been deeper otherwise I would have been in real trouble. The mangroves massive root system is very efficient at dissipating the actions of the tide, by slowing it down enough to deposit sediment on the waterbed, except for the finer particles which leave with the tide as it ebbs. We were surrounded by Red Mangrove, which live primarily in subtidal areas. Shortly after I jumped in, a small group of Spotted-eagle Rays turned up, I was not sure if they posed a threat or not, so to be on the safe side I opted to leave the water thankfully the silt was soft enough for me to extract myself with very little difficulty. The Rays were about one to two feet at their widest point, they appeared harmless enough, but you never know. We pushed on deeper into the mangroves, in doing so we were forced to abandon our paddles and use our hands to move forward. The channels had become very narrow indeed, to the point where our canoes were touching the bank on both sides.

We were making good headway when we encountered a Rufescent Tiger Heron, it was so close to us I could reach out and touch it. It adopted the typical Bittern posture of remaining perfectly still and bolt upright, beak pointing skyward with its eyes set in a way that it could see our every move as it looked down on us. It remained perfectly still in the belief that we would not see it; we let it continue to believe this and slowly drifted past, without spooking it. The rest of the day was spent searching for a way through the mangroves trying to reach our chosen start point on the map, in order to begin our search. Along the way we encountered many different birds we also saw Caiman's and a pretty cool Green Kingfisher that seemed as curious about us as we were about it. Every time we got close to it, it would move a short distance up stream, until it decided to fly off.

We eventually got to our start point by which time it was fast approaching four in the afternoon, so it was decided that we should find a place to make camp. There were three canoes in all, full of people and kit. We had to locate a good spot away from any potential danger, be it animal or flooding. We canoed through many channels until we broke into a large open area, which was dotted with small islands. We chose one of these islands for the night. It was ideal for setting up camp as it was quite high up and the tide mark only went halfway up the bank from the water's surface. We set up camp on this small isolated island, which was no bigger than fifty meters in circumference, before getting our heads down we thought it would be a good idea to paddle out into the middle of the open water. We drifted along surrounded by mangroves, then night fell, every now and then we would gently steer our canoes with our paddles. We laid there looking up at the night sky in wonder at the vast number of stars, there was no light or noise pollution. In response to the splashes we heard in the water, we would switch our torches on and catch glimpses of several pairs of eyes on the surface, we were careful not to put our hands in the water. I am not sure how long we drifted for, it felt like an eternity. Eventually we turned in for the night.

I lay awake in my Scratcher while the rest of the group were still pushing out the Z's (snoring). As I rested under the umbrella of a clear blue sky, all I could hear was the rustling of leaves as a gentle breeze passed over my face. I felt very snug in my sleeping bag. The dawn chorus was in full flow; the odd splash interrupted the chorus as a fish broke the surface of the water or was it a Caiman slipping beneath the surface. It really felt like I was all alone in the world, then in the distance I could hear a plane, its presence announced by the sound of its twin prop engines, the drone of the engines drew closer, and closer. I looked up and watched as it passed overhead. I felt like I wanted to get the pilots attention by jumping up and down, shouting and waving my arms just like you see in the films, but of course I knew they would not see let alone hear me. So, I stayed in my Gonk bag. The plane slowly disappeared into the distance; the fading sound of its engines gave way to the leaves rustling in the wind once more. As the outside world fell silent, the birds singing, the fish splashing, and the wind became the dominant sounds.

Once again, I felt as if I was alone in the world. 'In the Land that Time Forgot'. We set out after breakfast to begin cutting our way through the mangroves; as we were cutting our way through, there was a moment when I had the distinct feeling that this was the first time any human had ever stood on this part of the earth that we were on, of course I have no way of proving this. All I can tell you, it was a feeling that I had no reference to before nor since and given the huge vastness of the area and the fact that the locals did not venture into this area, I guess it is not surprising that no human had ever been there. The whole day was spent cutting into the mangroves, which oozed red blood like sap every time we drove our machetes into them. The cutting was easy going at first, but soon it became more difficult due of the density of mangroves we had to cut through. As a result, we had not moved very far at all, in fact we had covered less than fifty metres that day. We decided it was a fruitless task and set out back to basecamp.

We did not find the flamingos, perhaps it was a high goal for the bosses to have set us in the first place, but in terms of the adventure the whole experience was well worth having. There were lots of birds in and around the mangroves, two in particular were in abundance namely the Prothonotary and the Yellow-rumped Warbler or Yellow Butts as our American cousins like to call them. These warblers were mostly passing through on migration. I discovered later that the Prothonotary Warbler along with Lucy's Warbler are the only two new world warblers that nest in tree cavities: who would have thought it. I also discovered that Mangroves have many uses; they are melliferous, meaning that a bee can take nectar from the flower to make honey; the bark can be used as a source of tannins and dyes, the wood is also durable and water resistant and has been used to make houses and boats. The fruits and leaves can be eaten and drunk as a medicinal tea, so all in all a pretty good plant to have around.

The following week I and one of the admin staff a lady from Australia were driving south on the Hummingbird Highway and on this occasion my task was to recover one of our boats from Cary Cay which had broken down. On route I decided to stop for a rest by a river, of course birding as always was on the menu. I was hoping to see some Kingfishers and maybe a Flycatcher or two carrying out sorties across the river. The Cambridge English Dictionary definition of sortie is: 1. a short, quick attack by a military force, such as a small group of soldiers or an aircraft, made against an enemy position. 2. a short journey to somewhere you have not been before (which soldiers in the Falklands refer to as a Bimble), often with a particular purpose; or 3. an attempt to do something, and in the flycatcher's case it is without doubt to catch insects; often from a perch which is undercover.

I was sitting on the spare wheel of my Landrover relaxing and enjoying the sun when I was privileged to witness two hummingbirds interacting with each other in a courtship display; strictly speaking what they were doing was dancing with each other. I often share this experience with other birders; the only way to describe these hummingbirds is, imagine if you will, Diamonds, Rubies, Sapphires and Emeralds with wings. This is how these hummers appeared to me in that moment, which still does not do them justice, as they danced in and around me, at times inches away from my face; the hum of their wingbeats gently reaching my ears. Watching these magnificent birds was truly another one of nature's wonders.

At the halfway point we stopped at a garage on the intersection. I needed to arrange for a welder, as the trailer I was towing had snapped from the tow hook; I had managed to tie it together as a temporary solution. The reason the trailer broke was because the dirt road was full of ripples and the constant vibrations caused the trailer to give up the ghost. At one point I stopped to watch a Black Vulture eating a dead snake in the middle of the road. It was while we were at the garage we met with an English couple. As we chatted, they were telling me that they had decided to travel the world by bicycle, they had sold their house and everything else so they could fund their trip. They were looking for a way to cross the border south into Honduras. I suggested they head for Punta Gorda and hire a local to take them over by boat, or they could cross into Guatemala from Punta Gorda and drop down into Honduras from there.

Five Blues Lake is so described because of the different shades of blue the lake gives off; it is located at Mile 32 on the Hummingbird Highway. The lakes are thought to be around 200 feet deep and they are surrounded by ragged limestone hills, which are covered in a forest, consisting of broadleaf trees with scattered freshwater lagoons. It also boasts many spectacular caves and rock formations. The lagoons, caves and general area are still largely unexplored. I took the opportunity to visit the area during our return trip from recovering the boat and to drop off some much-needed supplies. It's an amazing place to explore, some 200+ birds and 20 species of bats have been recorded there. I went for a walk around one of the lakes where I came upon some of the cave systems, I did not go too deep into the caves as time was not on my side but I did explore a small cave system which broke out into a clearing What I encountered there was just fantastic. Above my head was a series of overhangs some 50-70 feet and on top of these overhangs there were trees growing. The limestone rock seemed strong enough to hold these tall trees and coming out from beneath of the over hangs were their roots, which drove straight down and were firmly rooted into the ground below. To get to the next cave system I had to negotiate the roots which were like tree trunks in themselves.

While out birding one day I came across a trail of Leafcutter Ants; I decided to sit and watch them for a while in the hope of bagging some new birds feasting on them as they went about their business, sadly it was not to be. I laid down beside their trail and watched the ants from ground level, what a privilege that was. One individual ant was carrying a leaf in its mandibles at least ten times its size and another much smaller cutter ant was riding on top of the leaf. I found out that its role was to fend off parasitic wasps. The trail they used was completely free from debris, it was as if someone had gone through the jungle with a large broom and had swept a path for them to move along more easily. I tried to relate what I observed to us humans, if we were able to do what they were doing.

I reckon it would be something like carrying a saloon car over my head with my best buddy riding on top of it, while walking down the M25 (Motorway) after having it swept clean first, and not even breaking into a sweat.

During our training camp phase, I had a lifer it was a really cool Vermillion Flycatcher. The males are a stunning red, with dark brown plumage; the females are similar to a Say's Phoebe. It was sitting on a fence post just outside our camp, surrounded by grassland, which is typical habitat for this small bird. This is when we met Winston, Belize's survival expert, he trained many British Soldiers including our

Special Forces. Winston is a walking encyclopaedia on how to survive in the jungle.

One time he told us about the thirty-second fruit, this was a fruit you would eat if you were constipated. He advised that it was important to adopt the position before eating it, if you ate it before assuming this position, you would have a clear understanding as to why it is called the Thirty-second Fruit. It really has to be said, that what Winston did not know about living off the land really was not worth talking about, or so I thought. I had planned to spend a week with him at the end of my tour with Raleigh International, I wanted to build on my survival skills on a 1-2-1 with him; sadly, he cancelled. He told me that a guy had walked in from Guatemala and told him that a shaman that lived up in the mountains had requested for Winston to visit him, as he had some important information to share with him. Winston said to me, that what this guy does not know about living off the land, really is not worth talking about and with that Winston walked into Guatemala with his mule, for god knows how long. It was a very humbling experience.

I went over to a bird filled place called Crooked Tree for some R&R, as a member of Raleigh International I got local rates as opposed to tourist rates, bargain. Directly outside my hut there was a hummingbird sitting on its nest; which was shaded by a large overhanging leaf, it was such a tiny thing. I have no idea which hummer it was, as I did not want to disturb it. During my stay there I took a boat trip with some Americans who were staying in the same camp. The son of the owner who took us, was a very knowledgeable birder. Later that night over a beer I was sitting with him and his father and we shared stories, I told them one that was told to me by someone in my unit about a Gurkha in Belize.

He was watching the Gurkha stalk a bird which was sitting on a post. He said that he stalked so slowly he reckoned that each step took well over a minute. When he got to within a few feet, he slowly reached out and lifted the bird off the post with one hand, amazing.

At the end of my tour, I took off to Guatemala to visit the Temples in Tikal. What an amazing place apart from all the fantastic birdlife, the temples were just awesome. While I was there, I managed to bag a Royal Flycatcher near to some tree covered Mayan earth mounds. The Flycatchers most notable feature is its long ornate crest, which is red to orange, with black and blue spots; the crest is usually recumbent. When fully erect, its flared laterally; they are known for fanning the crest when held in the hand, while rhythmically swaying the head from side to side somewhat like a wryneck. I climbed two of the temples, one was fifty metres high; the high steps made it difficult climbing indeed. Once at the top I had the most amazing view over the jungle canopy, it was a sea of varying shades of green, which was periodically broken by other pyramids reaching up through the canopy. It is well worth a visit if you are in the region.

On my return I caught the local bus to the nearest town, I had always wanted to travel that way, you know, on a bus packed with local people, chickens and goats sitting next to you. I rested my feet on some hessian sacks feeling disappointed to find that there weren't any chickens or goats on the bus. That was until the bus stopped; the sacks at my feet suddenly moved, and you've guessed it, chickens, the bags were full of chickens. The movement caused me to jump out of my skin, much to the amusement of the locals. I got off and as the bus drove away, I realised that I had left my Snowy River Hat on the stowage rack. It was a very expensive hat so I consoled myself with the thought that whoever found it had got themselves a really cool hat, or if they sold it, the money from the sale would feed their family, I like to think that they ate well.

The city of Palmas in the north eastern part of Brazil is where Tulio my guide collected me and took me to an Eco-lodge in Taquaruçu which is just a few hours out of the city. The owners of the eco-lodge had three dogs called Lucky, Thor, and Princesa. They also had a parrot called Carlota, every now and then she could be heard repeatedly saying the words "Macaco, Macaco, Macaco" which means monkey in Portuguese; the owner said that she lost her partner Napoleon, when they were attacked by monkeys, Napoleon was killed and eaten by them.

I spent three days searching for woodpeckers with great success. I bagged a Red-necked Woodpecker at its nest hole, a Yellow-tufted Woodpecker, a colourful woodpecker indeed, every morning it was right outside my bedroom and it would feed in the trees next to where I had my meals. An Ochre-backed Woodpecker; endemic to the region, was seen regularly while at the dinner table. I had two Plain-brown Woodcreepers displaying and copulating during one of my walks. Thor went ahead of me; when he stopped suddenly, his hackles were up, and he was growling. I did not see what he saw, it may have been a snake or a lizard. Whatever it was, it disappeared down a large hole. I was glad to have had him with me. It seems this is something he took upon himself to do, when a new group turned up, he did the same with them. Thanks to the Mighty Thor. On our days out we saw many birds from Burrowing Owl, Blue-crowned Trogon, to a pair of Sunbitterns which we bagged early hours in morning while it was still dark. We were on the way to find the Kaempfer's Woodpecker.

We saw Blue-and-yellow Macaws, Purple-throated Fruitcrow and Helmeted Manakin this was an amazing bird to watch, later on we had White-throated Woodpecker and at the end of that trip I spotted a Great-horned Owl way off in the distance, it was sitting on a rocky outcrop high up in the hills. It was so far away I could just about see it, it's droppings on the rockface gave it away.

I was dropped by boat deep in the Guyana jungle, clambering up the riverbank I surveyed the area I was in. I was looking for the best place to build my shelter; given the compactness of the jungle I decided the best course of action would be to stay close to the river. The risk of mosquito bites was increased. However, the upside was, I was close to water and a source of food; namely fish. I was on a survival course run by a former member of the SAS, having completed a week of training we were now on our own for the two-day isolation phase.

My shelter consisted of bamboo, palm leaves, and thin strips of vine used as cordage to tie it all together. I then set about collecting wood for my fire, thankfully it was not raining so I got my fire built, and lit quickly; in the process creating a lot of smoke, the aim was to drive away insects that might be lurking in and around my shelter, be it in the debris on the floor which was cleared away to the edge of the shelter or any that may be in the roof of my shelter. My tasks completed, I put a brew on, even though we were told not to take anything extra into the jungle. I am sorry, but a guy needs a cuppa when sitting by the bank of a river contemplating life, while waiting for a fish to take the bait. All the time I had an ear and eye out for any birds that were around. One of the first birds I saw was a Blue-throated Piping-Guan, it was perched deep within the trees along the river's edge, this large bird was difficult to see.

As night started to fall, I thought, I do not really want a Jaguar sneaking up on me in the night, so I decided to employ the cat/dog technique. From my shelter, I walked along the trail, while gripping my manhood; I sprayed the trees for twenty metres; the idea being that if anything did come down the trail, they would smell me before seeing me and hopefully my smell would be enough to put them off coming any closer. While I was very happy to see a Jaguar, I was just not up for any surprises while I slept. The next day was spent foraging for food, tending my fire, checking on my shelter, and of course birding as well.

Screaming Piha's, were sitting high up in the canopy, their loud call could be heard throughout the jungle, they had such a big sound for such a small bird. The second day, I went walkabout; after about fifty metres or so I could not see my campsite, fortunately I marked the reverse side of the trees with my machete along the way, which enabled me to retrace my steps back. Everything really did look the same, it would have been easy to get lost. At one point I found a small clearing where the sunlight broke through the canopy, I was soaking up the sun's rays when a Ringed Woodpecker came into view. It was foraging in and around the trees, searching behind the vines and along the branches of the middle story, a Western White-tailed Trogon was calling nearby, I love Trogons. On my return to camp, I brewed up, and as I relaxed drinking my tea, a Swallow-winged Puffbird made its way past my shelter.

It would stop now and then, turning its head through varying angles. It seemed to be checking me out, but in reality, it was probably searching for food and looking out for predators; it did not appear to be phased by my presence.

The first night was uneventful compared to the second night. I was laying in my shelter listening to the sounds of the jungle. My fire prevented me from looking out beyond it, past the firelight everything was black.

As I started to drift off to sleep, I heard a loud scream, whatever it was it ran off into the jungle. Its footfall was heavy and well-spaced apart, I concluded; it was probably a Tapir. I laid back on my bed and thought, looks like my strategy worked, one sniff of my piss and it was off. The next morning, I went down to the river to check on my line, my bait had gone, it was probably taken by a Payara – aka the Vampire Fish. A truly ferocious fish often described as a silver missile with an attitude; a fish with a strong demeanour and a face full of impressive daggers for teeth, in particular two huge fangs growing from its lower jaw that fit into nasal slots in their upper jaw. It is said that they literally hit the bait at speed and keep running like an express train on steroids.

Before night fell on the last day, we were extracted by boat and on the way back I decided to chance my arm at catching a Boa that was resting on one of the overhanging branches which lined the riverbank. The boat slowed beneath the half dozen or so young boas that were in this tree. I reached out and grabbed one of them, after a short while the Boa slipped free from my grip and bit me, (serves me right). I dropped it into the boat, and it disappeared under the equipment not to be seen again. Unlike the time in Gambia where one of the team leaders and I went to catch a Smiths-water Snake, which was hugging the river bank as it swam. As we approached it, we realised that it was in fact a Cobra; we retreated respectfully.

The next morning, I was up and birding. I managed to bag a female Golden-headed Manakin, a Crimson-crested Woodpecker and a flock of Red-throated Caracaras, they were making their way through the bush as one unit searching for prey. They seemed to be employing 'hit and run' tactics. Just then one of the local guides called out to me as he pointed skywards. I ran over and looked up; bagging my first King Vulture, as it glided across a clear blue sky, what an awesome lifer. After a short boat ride, we arrived at the Eco-Lodge, located inside the village of Surama. I had the chance to go birding with Ron the local bird expert, he showed me how to tell the differences between similar looking flycatchers, namely: Rusty-margined, Yellow-throated, Boat-billed, and Sulphury Flycatcher, Greater and Lesser Kiskadee, be it from the twitch of a tail to wing flicks or head movement, and of course song. During our short field trip, we entered a small copse, where we bagged a Great Potoo. It was just above our heads and was of course doing a great impersonation of a tree branch, another shapeshifter.

Often when I travel, I get taken for the Undertaker from the world wrestling federation, because it seems that I look like him, I say it is the other way round as I am older than he is, and it was no different when I visited Panama from Costa Rica. Arriving by boat I was walking along the jetty when someone called out "Undertaker", I said to him its fifty dollars for an autograph. Costa Rica was great, I could have spent more time there, I managed to bag Hoffman's, Black-cheeked and Pale-billed Woodpeckers and White-winged Manakin wing clapping. On another occasion I went on a zipwire trip for a good two to three kilometres through secondary jungle, I almost stepped on a Prague Nightjar and I had a great view of a Laughing Falcon. The next day I went birding on horseback; I saw loads of Three-toed Sloths, and that evening I was stoned by Howler Monkeys from the canopy.

CHAPTER 9

My Transition

B irding has had and continues to have a powerful impact on my life. Until recently I was unaware of how deep the healing power of birds can really go. I knew they had the power to heal, I just had not realised how powerful, not until I started to write this book. It started with a question that a close friend once asked, it was; why is it that I get very excited when I see woodpeckers, and even more excited when it's a new species of woodpecker, compared to the other lifers I have seen? This question caused me to reflect on past events that go way back into my childhood and the time I spent in boarding school.

I once gave a talk to the Institute of Outdoor Learning titled 'My Journey' where I mention that, nearly every major turning point in my life was made while I was connected to and with nature. Birds have been the one constant throughout my life, for example when I was struggling with my marriage I would go to the Zach and just sit there and watch the birds, at that time it was the one place I felt safe to be with my thoughts. There I could make sense of my life and those moments spent with the birds gave me clarity. I was able to explore my inner landscape in peace; versus the experiences of my external landscape. Nature and the Zach helped me to see the beauty in ugly, namely my ugliness.

The transition from civvy-street to the army was hard, but one I eventually learnt to manoeuvre through. The transition back into civvy-street was even harder. I had planned to stay in Germany where my children were living with their mother. However, seeing the lady crying at the side of the road in Bosnia had had a huge impact on me, more than I had realised at the time. After parking up in camp, I headed towards Regimental Headquarters (RHQ). Suddenly, I stopped, frozen to the spot for a few moments, in that moment I changed my mind about staying in Germany. I went into RHQ and spoke with the Chief Clerk. I told him I wanted to return to the UK for my last six months. God knows why, I never really liked being in the UK, in the 22 years I served the only time I went back there was for a course, and rarely on holiday, and yet here I was asking to go back. I could not get my head around it.

After returning to Germany some weeks later, I was walking down the main drag in camp, when again for some reason I stopped dead in my tracks. I saw myself surrounded by a high brick wall which towered way above me; and it was at least three bricks deep. I was trapped inside it, I experienced feelings of panic, my mind was rushing with thoughts of what am I going to do in the UK, I have nothing planned, I have no idea how the UK functions, I felt scared. If anyone had seen me, they would have thought that I had lost it. Then, the wall began to fall down, not brick by brick, but in large clumps of masonry, the wall represented my life and the 22 years I served. Each brick you could say represented a skill, or a lesson learnt throughout my life so far.

I looked around, wondering what the hell was going on, then it came to me. I had nothing to fear, I realised that I could choose to step over the rubble and go in any direction I wanted. I had the freedom to choose the direction in which I wanted to move forward with my life, I could choose new skills and new lessons to learn.

I was shown to my room in the Sgt's mess, I closed the door behind me, and I looked out of my bedroom window. I had what I now know was a panic attack, it scared the F%@king shit out of me. I started out here as a young gunner, and twenty-two years later I was back in Woolwich again. I did not take a year out, I took twenty-two. I was working in the resettlement office, and after a few weeks, I planned to take a trip to Belfast, with thoughts of moving back home. With my flight booked and my bags packed, I was really looking forward to going home. I turned up for work and got on with my tasks. Then around midday, I really lost it, I realised that I should have been on the plane winging my way home to Belfast, instead I went to work. I had forgotten all about my trip, and that night I struggled to sleep. The panic attacks, the sense of fear, the feelings of being lost, were to continue. During this time nature, and in particular birds were absent in my life.

One night, I left the pub having only had two beers. I was going back to my parents' house as I had moved in with them after leaving the army. It was dark, I was in a park, and I was crying, feeling desperate; I called out to the Big Fella, as I like to call the creator, for f&%k sake send someone to help me. From this point on I went on a journey of discovery. I realise now, that back then I must have been depressed. This was when I started to connect with myself spiritually, not religiously. I grew up in an environment of religious hatred and bigotry; this was something completely new to me. I could write a book about these experiences alone.

My connection with the Big Fella grew and grew, I was discovering my spirituality, and it seemed to move my life forward at a rate of knots, it was a real rollercoaster of a ride. I was finding a whole new me, a side of myself that lay dormant for most of my life, now I had a new toy to play with and to explore. I loved talking about it, until I realised many people could not hear what I was saying, I felt alone again. In the beginning there were no likeminded people to share my excitement with, but that was to change.

As I said before in Aldershot, I had two jobs, without any prior notice I informed work colleagues in each job that I was going to be sacked that day, you could say it was a kind of intuition that gave me the heads up on this. The first sacking hit me hard, really hard and even though I was out of the army and harm's way, you might say my baptism of fire into civilian life was intense to say the least; it was my first sacking after twenty-five years; it was traumatic.

Richard, who lived close by, came over to my place to support me, I was really grateful that he made time for me in my hour of need. Soon after, I took a job with Raleigh International; while working for them in Belize I discovered, I really wanted to work with people, realising I still had so much more to experience, and to give, it gave me a new sense of purpose. Sometime after my return I took a job in a rehab with a company called Promis, outside of the army, rehab was the best job

I have ever had, apart from the one I am doing now as a Nature-based Counsellor. Even when I was unwell, I so wanted to go to work. I loved it there and I learnt so much about myself and human behaviour. I was even allowed to take the clients into nature. I would take them through a series of nature awareness activities, the whole experience with these amazing people allowed me to develop my own approach to working with people in nature, which I call Natural Awareness. It gave rise to an understanding that was previously outside of my reach. It was a great honour to be with the people in rehab and I am grateful to all of them, especially to Dr Robert Lefever, for seeing something in me that I was still yet to discover.

Robert sponsored me through university – who would have thought it? As a young boy in boarding school I was called maladjusted, (some would say I still am), leaving school with no qualifications, getting into art college with no qualifications, and if you take away the qualifications I gained while serving in the army, the only academic qualification I have, is a Masters in Addiction Psychology and Counselling. Never in a month of Sundays would I have thought I would attend university, let alone qualify. On my first day at Uni I was ricocheting off the walls because the professors in my mind were speaking Russian and Chinese all rolled into one. I had not got a clue what they were talking about. However, life continued to be exciting and at times scary, but a good kind of scary. I soon discovered that there are many different aspects to connecting with nature and its healing power. I attended a bushcraft course run by Thomas Schorr-kon. Thomas was instrumental in helping me to make connections with past events in my life, things that I knew but did not have the language for; you could say he helped me to join certain dots together.

Everything felt like a breath of fresh air. I went on to train with Tom Brown Jnr in the USA which included nature connection, bushcraft and tracking. The latter I took to like a duck takes to water. I had had some previous experience in tracking while on my ILRRPS course. I attended Jon Young's Bird Language course in California, and another new window opened up for me as I began to see birds from another perspective. I was shifting into new realms of thinking, both personally, spiritually and professionally, and a lot of letting go had taken place along the way. Now, I no longer care about some things in the same way as I did before. Often, I am asked why I do not stick to the norm, in reality I don't think I ever have, I am happy in my skin, happy with who I am and who I can be. As I practised my nature connection and use of peripheral vision, I soon dropped using my scope when birding in favour of the bigger picture; I wanted to see what else was going on; was a crow dipping in flight to indicate the location of a potential predator? I would not have seen such an event with my eyes firmly fixed to my scope or bins for that matter. In turn the flip side of my transition was my spiritual growth; I became adept at looking at my bigger inner picture, without being distracted by my outer landscape.

I have discovered by using wilderness-living-skills, nature connection, bird language and tracking to help people connect with themselves through the power of nature; is a very rewarding experience indeed, even more so when my clients, nature and the Big Fella teach me something about myself that I had not seen before – what a gift!

In writing this book I have left a lot of detail out, I just wanted to give you an overview, there is so much more I could talk about; I will save that for another day. Suffice to say the transition from military to civilian life was extremely difficult; one that I had not prepared myself for. In military terms we would call this the 7 P's = Prior, Planning and Preparation, Prevents, Piss, Poor, Performance. Looking back, I actually went through quite a lot of difficult times, which were necessary in order for change to happen and happen it did. Sometimes, we need to come to the wall in order to see that we need to change direction.

The things said and done in the past were not wrong, they were all necessary and important, especially the ugliness and for that I am truly grateful, and long may it continue even when it seems scary. One thing is for sure, the one constant in my life has been and long may it continue to be:

More Birds Than Bullets...

CPSIA information can be obtained
at www.ICGtesting.com
Printed in the USA
LVHW051109030222
710036LV00009B/631